THE ARCHAEOLOGY OF
THE ROYAL FLYING CORPS

For Philip

THE ARCHAEOLOGY OF THE ROYAL FLYING CORPS

Trench Art, Souvenirs and Lucky Mascots

Melanie Winterton

Series Editor:
Nicholas J. Saunders

Modern Conflict Archaeology

Pen & Sword
MILITARY
AN IMPRINT OF PEN & SWORD BOOKS LTD.
YORKSHIRE · PHILADELPHIA

First published in Great Britain in 2022 by
PEN AND SWORD MILITARY
An imprint of
Pen & Sword Books Ltd
Yorkshire – Philadelphia

Copyright © Melanie Winterton, 2022

ISBN 978 1 39909 726 0

The right of Melanie Winterton to be identified as Author of this work has been asserted by her in accordance with the Copyright, Designs and Patents Act 1988.

A CIP catalogue record for this book is available from the British Library

All rights reserved. No part of this book may be reproduced or transmitted in any form or by any means, electronic or mechanical including photocopying, recording or by any information storage and retrieval system, without permission from the Publisher in writing.

Typeset in Times New Roman 11/13 by SJmagic DESIGN SERVICES, India.
Printed and bound in the UK by CPI Group (UK) Ltd.

Pen & Sword Books Ltd incorporates the imprints of Pen & Sword Archaeology, Atlas, Aviation, Battleground, Discovery, Family History, History, Maritime, Military, Naval, Politics, Social History, Transport, True Crime, Claymore Press, Frontline Books, Praetorian Press, Seaforth Publishing and White Owl

For a complete list of Pen & Sword titles please contact

PEN & SWORD BOOKS LIMITED
47 Church Street, Barnsley, South Yorkshire, S70 2AS, England
E-mail: enquiries@pen-and-sword.co.uk
Website: www.pen-and-sword.co.uk

Or

PEN AND SWORD BOOKS
1950 Lawrence Rd, Havertown, PA 19083, USA
E-mail: Uspen-and-sword@casematepublishers.com
Website: www.penandswordbooks.com

Contents

List of Figures vii
List of Plates ix
List of Tables xi
Acknowledgements xii
Modern Conflict Archaeology xiii
Prologue 1

Chapter 1	Setting the Scene 4
Chapter 2	Decoding the Evidence 10
	Matters of Air 10
	An Archaeology of the Senses 12
	Fear and Anxiety 14
	Trench Art and Souvenirs 15
Chapter 3	Being in a First World War Aeroplane 17
	Pilot and Aeroplane, a Haptic Engagement 19
	Adapting to the Extremes of Flying 20
	Pilot–Aeroplane Relationship 23
	Haptic Activities 25
Chapter 4	Reshaping the Aviator's Body and Mind 29
	Re-configuring the Human Body 29
	Re-configuring the Senses 30
	New Haptic Thresholds 35
	Communication 36
	Altering Cultural Perceptions of Time and Space 39
	Spatial Disorientation: Confusing the Senses 42
	Reflections on Flying the Conflict Body 43
Chapter 5	Mascots, Emotions, and Flying 45
	Defining a Mascot 46
	Lucky Mascots at the Beginning of the Twentieth Century 47
	Aviators and their Lucky Mascots 49

Chapter 6	The Surreal World of Flying 52
	Commercially Made, Sold as a Lucky Charm 52
	Personal Objects Infused with Special/Intimate
	Meaning Personal to the Aviator 58
	Lucky Pocket Pieces, Often with Survival Story 60
Chapter 7	Touching Magic: Omens and Ritual 64
	Lucky Sayings, Omens, and Rituals 64
	Objects Traditionally Associated with Good Luck in Folklore 68
	Charms with Religious Significance 69
	Belief, Action, and Objects 72
Chapter 8	Trench-art Propeller Grave Markers and the Stories they Tell 76
	Life Events of a Propeller Grave Marker 77
	Propeller Grave Markers as Trench Art, the
	Pre-acquisition Event 78
	Acquisition 81
	Manufacture 83
	Erection and Funeral 84
	Post-war Visitation 88
	Lost or Destroyed? 94
	Donation Elsewhere 96
	Discussion 98
Chapter 9	Souvenirs and Trench Art: Making Sense of Wooden Things 100
	Aviation-related Souvenirs: An Air War of 'Souveniring' 101
	Trench Art 103
Chapter 10	Memories of Linen and Metal: Souvenirs and Trench Art 112
	Linen 112
	Metal 117
	Conclusions 119
Chapter 11	How Time Flies 122
	Authenticity 122

Notes 124
Bibliography 142
Index 154

List of Figures

Figure 1: Saint-Omer airfield, France, 2012

Figure 2: Pilot and observer 'flying aces'

Figure 3: An observer demonstrating the precarious stance required to use the rear-facing Lewis gun, Sainte-Marie-Cappel, France, 1918

Figure 4: An aerial photograph. Area: River Ancre to River Somme. La Bassée Canal to River Scarpe

Figure 5: An interpretative sketch of the aerial photograph seen in Figure 4

Figure 6: A stereoscopic viewer and simple eye piece

Figure 7: The red devil mascot belonging to pilot Frank Bowles

Figure 8: Verso of the postcard describing FUMS UP!

Figure 9: An advertisement displaying three types of good-luck charms and mascots

Figure 10: A sketch by Francisque Poulbot detailing a street child playing with Nénette and Rintintin charms

Figure 11: RFC pilot Gerard Gwyn Crutchley

Figure 12: An example of the Lord's Prayer on a sterling silver disk to be worn on a chain

Figure 13: The propeller grave marker of 2nd Lieutenant John Hay, 40 Squadron, RFC, Aire Communal Cemetery, France

Figure 14: A trench-art letter opener crafted from the wooden propeller and engine strut of a Sopwith Pup aeroplane

Figure 15: A crashed German biplane with 'souveniring' Tommies

Figure 16: Wreckage of the German Gotha bomber shot down by Lieutenant Anthony John Arkell and Air Mechanic A.T.C. Stagg, 20 May 1918

Figure 17: The propeller grave marker of Lieutenant W.H. Ryder

Figure 18: The propeller grave marker of Brigadier General Gordon Shephard, with flower wreath from I Brigade

Figure 19: A German scout aeroplane brought down over Allied lines, Western Front, France

Figure 20: Civilians hunting in the grass for German bullets and other souvenirs of the war, Senlis, northern France

Figure 21: Lieutenant H.C. Cutler in his car in 1916

Figure 22: A shot-down German Fokker biplane, Cambrai front, France.

Figure 23: Major William Barker standing in front of Sopwith Camel B6313

List of Plates

Plate 1: A popular postcard

Plate 2: A postcard from the Fum's Up! set, Oilette Series Postcard No. 8792A

Plate 3: Sterling silver Fum's Up! charm, circa 1914

Plate 4: Examples of Nénette, Rintintin, and a baby

Plate 5: RFC pilot charm presented as trench art, constructed in the image of a Handley Page O/400 aeroplane

Plate 6: Sunny Jim

Plate 7: The front side of a First World War USAAS pilot's religious charm

Plate 8: The rear side of a First World War USAAS pilot's religious charm

Plate 9: A 3-D model of a monoplane made from gold-coloured metal, produced in 1916

Plate 10: A rounded brass plaque with a pair of pilot's brevets engraved at the top, attached to the propeller grave marker of 2nd Lieutenant John Hay, No. 40 Squadron, RFC

Plate 11: A fragment of tin funeral wreath plaque, 2nd Lieutenant John Hay, No. 40 Squadron, RFC

Plate 12: A row of four RFC graves, Terlincthun British cemetery, Wimille, France

Plate 13: A trench-art biplane with twin propeller blades, stamped 'Ypres'

Plate 14: The propeller grave marker of Lieutenant Herbert Cecil Cutler

Plate 15: A section of a wooden propeller blade with a painted scene depicting an RFC aeroplane flying through anti-aircraft explosions

Plate 16: A trench-art-style photograph frame with photographs of an unknown serviceman and his friends and family, made from the wooden propeller tip of a First World War aeroplane

Plate 17: A trench-art propeller clock from the archive stores of the Shuttleworth Collection

Plate 18: A trench-art model of a biplane with a four-bladed propeller

Plate 19: A trench-art model of a biplane with a two-bladed propeller

Plate 20: A trench-art letter opener

Plate 21: A trench-art button hook

Plate 22: An RFC button, used to personalize the trench-art letter opener and button hook

List of Tables

Table 1: Aviators' lucky mascots, omens, sayings, and rituals: categories of superstition

Table 2: Events of social interaction in the social life of a propeller grave marker

Table 3: Samples of cemeteries in France and Belgium containing the graves of First World War aviators, visited by the author in 2012

Acknowledgements

I did not just sit down and somehow produce this book; it involved a lot of research and, during that research, I received much help. I visited numerous institutions to delve in their archives, making salient notes as I did so. Of these institutions I would wholeheartedly like to offer my sincere gratitude to the staff at the Imperial War Museum London, the RAF Museum London, and the Shuttleworth Collection at Old Warden Aerodrome, Bedfordshire. Their assistance, time, patience, enthusiasm, and professionalism is very much appreciated.

On a personal level I would like to extend my heartfelt gratitude to Andrew Kemp of Cross and Cockade International, Colonel (Retd) Stamford Cartwright, Curator of the Collection, Worcestershire Yeomanry Museum, and Gerry Crutchley for their generosity in providing photographs. In addition, I wish to say thank you to the team at Pen & Sword. In particular, to Rupert Harding for commissioning my book and to Alison Flowers for a thorough and professional edit.

A huge thank you also is due to Professor Nicholas Saunders who invited me to write this book for Pen & Sword's Modern Conflict Archaeology series. He not only introduced me to modern conflict archaeology (I was always adamant that prehistory, particularly the Neolithic and Bronze Age periods, were my areas of interest and specialism) but I somehow changed direction to study modern conflict archaeology and he became my PhD supervisor and mentor introducing me to books that made me view the world and its objects from new and interesting perspectives.

Finally, many thanks to my husband, Philip, who encouraged me to write this book.

Modern Conflict Archaeology

THE SERIES

Modern Conflict Archaeology is a new and interdisciplinary approach to the study of twentieth and twenty-first century conflicts. It focuses on the innumerable ways in which humans interact with and are changed by the intense material realities of war. These can be traditional wars between nation states, civil wars, religious and ethnic conflicts, terrorism, and even proxy wars where hostilities have not been declared yet nevertheless exist. The material realities can be as small as a machine-gun, as intermediate as a war memorial or an aeroplane, or as large as a whole battle-zone landscape. As well as technologies, they can be more intimately personal – conflict-related photographs and diaries, films, uniforms, the war-maimed and 'the missing'. All are the consequences of conflict, as none would exist without it.

Modern Conflict Archaeology (MCA) is a handy title but is really shorthand for a more powerful and hybrid agenda. It draws not only on modern scientific archaeology, but on the anthropology of material culture, landscape, and identity, as well as aspects of military and cultural history, geography, and museum, heritage, and tourism studies. All or some of these can inform different aspects of research, but none are overly privileged. The challenge posed by modern conflict demands a coherent, integrated, sensitized yet muscular response in order to capture as many different kinds of information and insight as possible by exploring the 'social lives' of war objects through the changing values and attitudes attached to them over time.

This series originates in this new engagement with modern conflict and seeks to bring the extraordinary range of latest research to a passionate and informed general readership. The aim is to investigate and understand arguably the most powerful force to have shaped our world during the last century – modern industrialized conflict in its myriad shapes and guises, and in its enduring and volatile legacies.

THIS BOOK

A key element of Modern Conflict Archaeology is the anthropological exploration of the senses and its connections to material culture. Arguably nowhere is this better seen than in the new conflict dimension of the air – the contested airscape – hitherto unconquered by humans, but between 1914 and 1918 explored and dominated by aircraft made of wood, linen and glue. This was a revolutionary development, not least in its associations with aerial photography, surveillance, mapping, and bombing, and in its contribution to the decline of the millennia-old role of cavalry in battlefield reconnaissance. But, whilst there are many books on First World War aircraft technology, development, tactics, and weaponry, the sensual world of these first aviators has been largely absent. The physical and psychological challenges of flying in a fragile open-cockpit aeroplane in a new and hostile domain, whether for fighting or observation, and without parachutes, have only now been documented and analysed from the perspective of the senses and how these sensual aspects were materialized in physical objects such as mascots.

Melanie Winterton's research over the last decade has transformed our knowledge and understanding of the sensual experiences of these young pilots and charted how different flying was then compared with today. Her doctoral thesis and publications have revealed a rich new area for interdisciplinary investigations – gathering together evidence and insights scattered across innumerable sources and applying a powerful modern focus and theoretical analysis to their understanding.

In this book, Melanie has written a well-crafted accessible account of pilot experiences, exploring previously under-recognized aspects of how the human body adapts and copes with the unrelenting stress and dangers of fighting modern wars. She shows how items such as lucky mascots, souvenirs, trench art, and transient sayings and actions are linked to spiritual, religious, and superstitious beliefs. The bringing together of such disparate aspects of the often very short lives of First World War pilots opens a startling window on modern aerial conflict – its anthropological and archaeological dimensions – and which complement the knowledge and understandings of traditional aerial military history.

We are taken on a journey, a flight of interdisciplinary adventure and importance, where the effects of freezing temperatures combine with memories of loved ones, where memoirs and diaries not only record events but are themselves sensual objects. We feel the discomfort of young men fitting into their cockpit seats, fighting dizziness, gasping for breath, deftly moving their joysticks, feeling the resistance of the wind, and searching the sky for telltale signs of enemy aircraft. We glimpse the short-lived world of mutual gentlemanly respect between pilots of opposing airforces, of dashing aces, famous aircraft, and ingenious aerial manoeuvres.

Importantly, we see too how the physical legacies of those who did not survive the war were often as distinctive as the combat lives they had lived. Wooden propeller grave markers along the Western Front were a prominent visual presence in the immediate aftermath of the war years, only disappearing when replaced by the standard Portland stone headstones of the Imperial (now Commonwealth) War Graves Commission. How many of these were destroyed, simply tossed aside in a war cemetery's rubbish dump in France or Belgium – and how many became memorials to the dead taken back home becoming a shrine, or ending up on the wall of a local church or cathedral? And the large and the small could sometimes sit side by side reinforcing each other's message of personal loss. Small model aircraft made of bullet cartridges, scrap brass, and shells are a common feature of trench art. The secret and emotionally distressing lives of such objects are just one of the little-known aspects of the aerial war of 1914–1918 that the author introduces us to and then guides us through with expert eyes.

This is a landmark book because it tells previously untold stories in light of new ways of looking at objects and their relationships with people, places, and events, and the heightened sensibilities of our age. It focuses on the author's rich and detailed research, is illuminated by her own experiences of flying in an open cockpit aircraft, of visiting numerous museums, and possessing a deep emotional resonance with her subject. It carves a new path for others to follow in all the aerial wars which came after 1918, and which too often are underplayed in favour of recounting the terrestrial events. This is a book about how it feels to be a human being in a contested airscape in all its drama, excitement, and dread.

Nicholas J. Saunders
University of Bristol, July 2022

'The material world shapes and transforms us . . . It shapes our sensory experiences, our emotional responses, our social organisation . . . and our understanding of the world.'

Nicole Boivin, Material Cultures, Material Minds. The Impact of Things on Human Thought, Society, and Evolution*, 181*

'To see [a pilot] at his best [you] would have to accompany him, through the storm of the anti-aircraft guns, into those fields of air where every moment brings some new trial of the quickness of his brain and the steadiness of his nerve. He is now in the workshop where tradition is made, to be handed down as an heirloom to the coming generations.'

Sir Walter Raleigh, 1922

Prologue

I enjoy nothing better than whiling away a few hours in an aeroplane museum. In the 1980s, I lived in the Colindale-Hendon area of North London and was a frequent visitor to the RAF Museum and continue to visit to this day when an indulgent trip to London permits. Other favourites are the Imperial War Museum, Duxford; the Shuttleworth Collection, Old Warden Aerodrome, Bedfordshire; Stowe Maries Great War Aerodrome, near Maldon, Essex; and the Army Flying Museum, Middle Wallop, Hampshire. In addition, if your aerial interest extends to helicopters, I also recommend the Helicopter Museum in Weston-super-Mare.

Walking past the aeroplane exhibits, I am not particularly enthusiastic about reading interpretation boards that detail the size of the engine or the date it was made or even how fast it flew – I know many are (including my husband). Indeed, when visiting a museum with my husband we always split up to walk round the exhibits and, if questioned after the visit, it is likely that it would appear as if we had visited different museums. Of course, it is wonderful that we all have different outlooks on the world and this book relates to aspects that capture my imagination and research interests.

The First World War aeroplanes themselves are an important focus of consideration. Some of them have become museum exhibits and, although they have been cosmetically retouched, or completely rebuilt, they are no longer operational. At the RAF Museum London there is a replica of a Bristol F.2B Fighter, E2466, representative of the aeroplane flown by Captain William Harvey, No. 22 Squadron, exhibited within the confines of an area cordoned off with rope informing the visitor that you can look but you must not touch. It is a beautiful thing to behold and I have to prevent myself from reaching out to touch it. Sadly.

In controlling viewers' senses in terms of forcing their gaze, the opportunity to touch the aeroplane is denied, as is the chance to connect the past with the present. However, the viewer, the museum visitor, could mentally engage with the aeroplane, mentally probe the tactile world, imagine all sorts of scenarios and ask copious questions, which would, of course, remain unanswered. How do I climb in? Will I fit in the cockpit? Would my legs feel cramped? What would it feel like to fly it? What are the chances of falling out? What would things look like from above? Would I feel apprehensive or anxious flying in such a flimsy aeroplane? Would I feel the wind on my face? Would it be noisy? Would I feel travel sick? Would I be able to breathe easily? Would I register that the aeroplane was moving?

Many of these questions can be answered by flying in an open-cockpit aeroplane which is why I elected to experience what it was like to fly in one as an element of the fieldwork undertaken to research and write this book.[1] Of course, we can attend those magnificent Flight Display Days at, for example, Old Warden Aerodrome, Bedfordshire to see First World War aeroplanes fly and to hear their engines, but we do not get to fly them, we do not get to comprehend what it felt like to fly in an open-cockpit biplane, to feel the wind against one's face. No First World War service personnel are alive today, so first-hand participant observation of flying 100-year-old biplanes is impossible, though modern replicas and somewhat younger biplanes of the 1930s is as near as one can get to appreciating their experiences between 1914 and 1918. Participant observation and perception is adopted as a means of comprehending the sensory experience of being in an open-cockpit biplane. It contributes an element of authenticity and empathy.

My approach, therefore, is 'auto-ethnographical' in terms of experiencing the technology of another era to see how First World War pilots might have related to the aviation technology available at that time.[2] Personal experience is integral to archaeological-anthropological research. This approach permitted a degree of immersion in and comprehension of the sensorium within which First World War pilots flew, though clearly not the anxiety and stress produced by combat. My observations and feelings about the flight were written up in a field notebook to account for the phenomenological reality of the way my work was produced. This added an element of personal experience to my research enabling me to understand flying terms so that the witness accounts of First World War pilots could be better interpreted.

The replica Bristol F.2B Fighter exhibited at the RAF Museum London is constructed from the parts of six aeroplanes. This fact acted as a catalyst to my thinking. Many First World War aeroplanes, when engaged in conflict, incurred severe damage to, for example, both fuselage and wings which affected their ability to fly for they 'could be . . . pierced in 50 places, missing the occupants by inches (blissfully unaware of how close it had come until they returned to base)'. Often such damage could be quickly fixed and the wings could be patched with small pieces of linen painted with dope.[3] All well and good, but many First World War aeroplanes crashed; whilst those that could be were repaired, what happened to those that were beyond saving, what happened to all the smashed bits and pieces? In addition, how did an aviator cope with the constant threat that his fragile aeroplane could break up in the sky at any time?

To answer this, a modern conflict archaeology approach, a hybrid of anthropology and archaeology, has been adopted to write this book because it allows us to focus on the relationships between culture and the material worlds of the recent past, providing the tools to explore areas that remain unaddressed by, for example, history, battlefield archaeology, and aviation excavation. As an object of war, an aeroplane represents visceral personal experiences. First World War aeroplanes possess value as anthropological-archaeological objects through their cultural association and legacies. Such legacies are enduring because material memories of these aircraft survive in people's homes, in museums, as photographs, and as mentions in aviators' written memoirs and diaries, creating new perspectives on the conflict as they follow different trajectories and create varying relationships with those with whom they come into contact. As these physical remains become modern heritage, modern conflict archaeology allows us to focus on the reification of relationships between individuals, culture, and the material worlds of wartime experience and post-war memory.

We perceive and experience our environment through our senses. Nevertheless, it is not until recently that anthropologically grounded interdisciplinary questions have been asked about how the human senses respond to conflict in the air. In applying such an approach that incorporates experiential, sensorial, agentive, and biographical considerations to the study of First World War aviation, it is intended that this book will contribute to a more detailed and nuanced appreciation of human relationships with aviation technology, how the aviators created depth and dimension in their social worlds, and how their experiences and emotions were materialized in a range of objects – in trench art, souvenirs, and lucky mascots.

Melanie Winterton
July 2022

Chapter 1

Setting the Scene

Only a few years before the outbreak of the First World War, brothers Orville and Wilbur Wright had made four flights – on 17 December 1903, at Kittyhawk, North Carolina – in the first heavier-than-air fixed-wing aircraft powered by a small petrol engine. Such fledgling technology offered a new form of sensorial engagement with a world in the air. In 1914, flying was, therefore, a recent and pioneering corporeal experience. Numerous young men went from a world of bicycles, horses, carts (and occasionally motor cars) to joining the Royal Flying Corps (RFC). From reading the letters, diaries, and books written by these men, it is clear that they joined for different reasons – whether a patriotic desire to fulfil their sense of duty, or simply the excitement of pursuing an adventure, and often both.

Pilot Hugh Granville White described in his diary how his interest in flying harked back to 1909 whilst attending Preparatory School in Eastbourne. He recalled how the school's playing fields provided the perfect place for flying model aeroplanes which had become a very popular and fun pastime for young boys. His model aeroplane had been a much-cherished birthday present. He remembered that it was a tractor biplane made from wood and red silk and '[a]lthough it never flew very well, it managed to cover quite a good distance before crashing (which never did it much harm)'.[1]

Pilot Douglas Sholto was later to write: 'a poem by Maurice Baring entitled "Per Ardua, 1914–1918" contains a delightful line about the first squadrons of the Royal Flying Corps setting out for France "as gaily as to a dance". That strikes just the note of the mood in which so many of us went off to war.'[2]

For Australian Gordon Taylor, flying during warfare was the preferred option over trench warfare for an 'aeroplane offered a means of individual expression [and] a man could to some extent control his own destiny'.[3] First World War pilot Harold Balfour wrote that he was often asked whether it was more agreeable to be in the RFC or the infantry which he thought to be a pointless question as the choice is down to personal preference but 'the difference and the advantage of life in the Flying Corps was that we had three or four hours each day of intense fear, but that the rest of the time we lived in the utmost comfort'.[4]

Recognizing that the work of the cavalry for reconnaissance-at-a-distance was increasingly redundant, the British Directorate of Military Operations was quick to understand the advantages aviation could bring.[5] The Royal Flying Corps was created by Royal Warrant on 13 April 1912, becoming established in May 1912. It consisted of three independent wings – Military (Royal Flying Corps), Naval (Royal Naval Air Service), and a Central Flying School for training pilots.[6] The RFC's motto is *per ardua ad astra*, 'through adversity to the stars'.

Pilots in the RFC were divided into tactical units called squadrons. Pilots came from across the world to fly in the First World War – Canada, United States of America, New Zealand, Australia, and South Africa – often meeting for the very first time in the huts they stayed in during training as cadets:

> There are twenty men to a flight, and in our case they are a pretty cosmopolitan crew. Most of the colonials answer to their country's name. A big Columbian opposite me is known as 'Canada', another is 'Algiers'. A man from Cape Town has been abbreviated down to 'SA', and I am known as 'Australia'.[7]

On 1 April 1918, the Royal Flying Corps and the Royal Naval Air Service (RNAS) merged to form the Royal Air Force (RAF), now independent of the British Army and under the control of the new Air Ministry.[8]

The pioneering skills and courage of pilots made flying appear exciting, attracting young men, like Arthur Gould Lee, to join the RFC at the outbreak of war. Heading for the No. 1 Aircraft Depot at Saint-Omer, France, the destination of most squadrons deployed to the Western Front and the gateway to France for replacement aircraft and pilots who were posted to units across France and Belgium, pilot Arthur Gould Lee remembered sending a postcard home from the Hotel Folkstone at Boulogne where he was billeted: 'there was nothing much to say except that the sea was rough, and everybody including me, was hopelessly sick. Not the cleverest way to celebrate the first time I've been out of England, nor, for that matter, my formal entry into my first war.'[9]

Saint-Omer was the site of the largest airfield on the Western Front and was occupied continuously throughout the First World War by over fifty RFC squadrons and was also the site of a large aircraft repair and storage depot. The Headquarters of the RFC was also in Saint-Omer where a night out on the town was a regular social event for members of the RFC. Today, the site of the airfield, although still an aerodrome, is devoid of signs of such hustle and bustle (see Figure 1).

A memorial commemorating the members of the British Air Services and air forces from every part of the British Empire who served on the Western Front from 1914 to 1918 was erected in Saint-Omer in 2004 by Cross and Cockade, the First World War Aviation Historical Society, to mark the ninetieth anniversary of the

Figure 1. *Saint-Omer airfield, France, 2012.* (© Author)

first RFC aircraft to arrive at Saint-Omer. Since memory is cultural, the memory of the British Air Services has been attributed meaning through the erection of the memorial.[10] However, such memorials often omit the experiences of those being remembered, for 'in every memorial, something has been left out or forgotten . . . the omission or exclusion of the pain and horror of war on those memorials'.[11] Through paying a mark of respect to the young men, we should know of their experiences especially now that all people who served in the First World War have passed on and such memorials are reduced to sites of memory.

This book focuses on the aviators' experiences and relationships with objects whilst serving on the Western Front, the main theatre of war during the conflict. It spans over 400 miles of trenches and stretches from the dunes of the West Flanders Belgian coast in the north to the frontier crossing at the village of Pfetterhouse on the Swiss-German (Alsace) border in the south. Experiences of aviators on the Home Front are also included, though to a lesser extent.

Up until March 1917, aviators in the RFC who undertook reconnaissance duties were regarded as the eyes of the army, adding another dimension to the war on the ground (see Plate 1) as the field of vision was extended.

Aerial photography was a fledgling development and aviators risked their lives to take photographs as battlespace was extended to the air. Low oblique photographs were very difficult to take because the aeroplane had to be flown closer to the ground exposing the aviator to enemy fire. In terms of archaeology, such photographs are a potent legacy of the First World War. O.G.S. Crawford, an observer in the RFC, was so impressed with the possibilities of air photography in locating and identifying archaeological sites, that he was instrumental in introducing it to landscape archaeology. Indeed, after the war, Crawford worked at the Ordnance Survey in Southampton where aerial images, checked and supplemented by fieldwork, were employed to revise the archaeological information on the Ordnance's maps.[12]

It was not until 1917 that aerial combat became a means of waging war in the skies and flying aces became the heroes of the day, the public admiring the death-defying feats undertaken during dogfights.[13] 'The great McCudden . . . just back from the front to get decorated again, came into Murrays last night for dinner . . . what a riot he caused. . . . women fought to get at him.'[14] It is perhaps these flying individuals (see Figure 2) who are remembered most, because the public 'preferred a romantic, glamorous version of the pilot's war to the truth of the fearful days he had known'.[15]

Figure 2. *The text on the back of this photograph labels every pilot and observer pictured a 'flying ace', 'having brought down at least three enemy aircraft'.* (Author's collection)

In reality, from the outbreak of war until at least March 1917, there were no flying aces, for the young men of the RFC carried out the routine duties of photography, reconnaissance, artillery observation, bombing, and protective fighter patrols.

Few aviators, if any, kept a specific record of their sensorial experiences, although Australian pilot Geoffrey Wall wrote a description of his first flight in a letter home: 'I opened the throttle a bit and started trundling across the short grass, quite slowly at first, for, as a bit of an epicure in sensation, I wanted to study my experiences'.[16] It is clear that aviators' diaries and books are littered with references which can now be re-valued as evidence of their sensorial engagement with objects large and small. Duncan Grinnell-Milne wrote about learning to fly, referring to it as 'the puzzling business of aviation'. He describes how he:

> . . . had to study the air. The wind must be a certain strength, the clouds at a given height and of known density . . . I must learn how to sniff the air like an old hound, a flying hound; to judge the quality of the atmosphere from the wind upon my cheek.[17]

RFC Observer Alan Bott's book brings to life the quotidian experiences of the flying officer in France. Bott was very much aware of the relationships that were formed between aircrew and their aeroplanes. For example, he observes that 'each man treated his bus as if it were an only child' because '[i]f another pilot were detailed to fly it the owner would watch the performance jealously, and lurid indeed was the subsequent talk if an outsider choked the carburetter [*sic*] taxied the bus on the switch, or otherwise did something likely to reduce the efficiency of engine or aeroplane'.[18]

Keeping diaries was forbidden, and so they too were contested 'objects'. Wartime publications were heavily anonymized, for example, Aimée McHardy's book, written using letters received from her husband, fighter pilot William Bond, whilst serving in France during 1917, was subject to heavy censorship and the names of Bond's fellow airmen and locations were redacted.[19] Another example is the book written by Alan Bott, referred to above, which was originally published under the pseudonym of 'Contact' and even his squadron was disguised by the name 'Umpty' Squadron, such were the publishing restrictions of the time.[20]

Aviators kept diaries for different reasons. Lieutenant Colonel L.A. Strange, for example, hoped, '[i]f these recollections help only to show the futility of war amongst nations my purpose is served'.[21] An 'anonymous American aviator', whom we now know to be John McGavock Grider, visualized a future after the war, 'I'll read parts of it to my grandchildren'.[22] He gave his diary to a fellow officer, Elliott White Springs, asking him to publish it in the event of his death – he was fatally shot down behind enemy lines during the closing months of the war and buried by the Germans.[23]

Interestingly, whilst few diaries were published many were donated to museum archives along with private documents such as letters and photographs. Lieutenant Lidsey's diary was given to the Imperial War Museum by his brother who included the following addendum:

> This is a copy of the diary kept by my brother William John (Jack) – written daily – almost – in pencil in 4 cheap pocket notebooks, and records the daily events during his service in the 1914–1918 war until the date of his death from wounds received the previous day in March 1917 . . . I think it is valuable for future generations in showing the truly appalling physical conditions which were endured by ordinary human beings for months and years on end without a breakdown of morale.[24]

It was not only well-educated officers who kept diaries. James McCudden VC was a leading British fighter pilot of the First World War whose personal account was completed just days before his death in July 1918, aged 23. His book was published posthumously.[25] He had left school at 14 years of age, impressively rising from mechanic to pilot to flight commander in a short space of time.

Turning to the authenticity of the books and diaries that the aviators wrote, I have taken them at face value as being honest and true individual witness accounts. Indeed, Observer Alan Bott brings to life the quotidian experiences of the flying officer in France.[26] The introduction to his book is written by Major General Brancker who comments that Bott wrote about 'heroic deeds with such moderation and absence of exaggeration' and this is the spirit that I have followed.[27] Such written accounts are however *versions* of reality that fossilize interpretations. Their true value is that they are the product of genuine aviators but that does not necessarily mean that all they contain is true and an element of critical caution is required. Nevertheless, these sources are as near to 'authentic' as we can get.

Chapter 2

Decoding the Evidence

Given the complexity and interdisciplinary nature of the research presented in this book, I have employed a variety of theoretical approaches – experiential, sensorial, agentive, and biographic – from the hybrid discipline of material culture studies. In adopting a material culture approach, I move beyond the processual paradigms that analysed the form, materials, and method of manufacture of an object and cast aside Cartesian dualisms of object and person. Material culture studies 'centres on the idea that materiality is an integral dimension of culture, and that there are dimensions of social existence that cannot be fully understood without it'.[1] This position offers a powerful and fruitful way of investigating aviators' haptic experience of flying, use of lucky mascots, individuality in creating, or getting somebody else to create, trench art, which became repositories for human experience and memory objects.

Matters of Air

Chapters 3 and 4 describe what it was like for a First World War pilot to fly in the air – but also to address what is air and how can we think about it in an anthropological sense? Steven Connor explores the ways in which the scientific understanding of the air 'has both given rise to new kinds of object and made of the air itself a new kind of object . . . a new way of being an object'. Connor tells us how the domestication of air is the product of scientific invention, for example, fireworks in the UK to mark Guy Fawke's night and the invention of high explosives following the discovery of nitroglycerine in 1847. He explores a variety of artefacts from examples of contemporary art to the scientific observation of atmospheric phenomena through a series of encounters with air from the late sixteenth century onwards starting with 'the process of experimental investigation into the mechanics of air . . . along with the pneumatic chemistry that . . . may be said to begin with Van Helmont's coining of the word "gas" in the early seventeenth century'. Connor concerns himself with 'the ways in which new understanding of the air entered social experience and altered human experiences of their ways of inhabiting the world'. He also writes of developments in military technology, such as poison gas and aerial bombardment that 'made more and more for "an air that kills"'.[2]

My research draws on but seeks to go beyond Connor's because it deals with humans taking to the air voluntarily and in powered flight for the first time. Industrialized war made this possible and so before 1914 Connor's question is philosophical, but afterwards air presents itself to direct human experiences via the technology of flying. Underpinning this book also is the issue of haptics (the senses of touch) as an interpretive framework to discover what it felt like to fly in a contested air space in an open-cockpit biplane.

The development of powered flight provided an important means of occupying or moving through the air, particularly in the extremes of aerial combat. To offer new analytical understandings of air, this book explores how air as a cultural medium was first defined and then refined by First World War aviators' experiences of flying over the Western Front, and how it became part of their haptic experiences.

Studies of air have primarily been a means of researching our relationship with the environment. For example, for cultural history, Peter Sloterdijk regards the First World War as an environmental conflict where the atmosphere became a theatre of war, where the air was reconfigured as a weapon. On 22 April 1915, the German Army first used chlorine gas at Ypres, in Belgium, and the air became an instrument of atmo-terrorism.[3] This forced soldiers to breathe in toxic 'weaponized' air that would seriously injure or kill them. Fresh air could no longer be taken for granted.

In re-thinking the human body's relationship with technology, Bruno Latour argues that nobody knew that air was part of the body's sensorial spheres until the Germans released these deadly gases into the air in 1915.[4] However, air alone is insufficient – it requires movement for Sloterdijk's argument to work – so the German use of gas required wind, and blowing from the right direction. It is true, as Sloterdijk says, that chemical warfare attacks a human's ecologically dependent vital functions such as respiration, central nervous system, and temperature.[5] But it is also true that First World war aviators also reconfigured 'air' as a medium to attack and kill. Pilots similarly had to deal with vital functions of breathing, temperature, and central nervous system episodes of, for example, disorientation and blackouts.

Sloterdijk's insights are significant, but serve also as a jumping-off point for further elaboration, critique, and analysis in light of pilots' First World War experiences. Sloterdijk's assertion that chemical warfare supersedes traditional/ naïve exchange of blows between enemies is surely only partly true as demonstrated in this book, where pilots not only have to deal with the sensory assault, but the aim is not to make the exchange of blows redundant, but to more effectively deliver them through aerial combat, strafing, and bombing.[6]

A similar critical comment can be levelled at Sloterdijk's description of gas masks/respirators as a quickly created/refined counter-measure to gas, yet fails to mention the visual and breathing problems associated with wearing them, and thus successfully navigating the physical landscapes of combat terrain.[7] It is also the case, unacknowledged by Sloterdijk, that pilots too wore helmets, goggles, and, when flying high, employed oxygen masks. It can be argued that whilst chemical warfare is a vital development in the weaponization of 'air', as Sloterdijk says, he overplays his hand, and really it is only part of this process (albeit extreme and illegal and morally repugnant) which really began with the invention/use of aircraft.[8] After all, aircraft attacks of all kinds have killed more people (soldiers and civilians) in the First World War and subsequent twentieth-century conflicts than gas attacks. Aircraft can fly/attack/kill in many wind conditions, whereas gas attacks need a very particular set of wind conditions if users are not to kill their own side.

An Archaeology of the Senses

To understand what we mean by 'the senses', it is useful to look at the history of their study for it is clear that philosophers of science have evidently speculated on the matter of how we perceive our world since long before the advent of formal scientific disciplines. The number and orders of the senses are fixed by custom and tradition.[9] In Aristotle's hierarchy of the five traditional senses – (1) sight; (2) hearing; (3) smell; (4) taste; and (5) touch – he places 'touch' at the bottom attributing it to the sense of an animal, whilst privileging sight as the most developed human sense.[10] Thus Greek tradition, in separating mind and body, regarded the mind as being superior to the body in that animals had senses but humans had intellect. In reality it is not known how many senses we have but Rivlin and Gravelle indicate that we may have more than five sensory systems.[11] Recognition of the five separate senses remains evident today, although a more realistic framework for interpreting sensory experience is surely to acknowledge that all sensory experience is *multi-sensorial*.[12] However, we may still focus on single senses in pursuit of the non-obvious, although no one sense could ever tell the whole story.

At this point I would like to introduce the American psychologist James Gibson who is particularly known for his theory on 'affordances'. This takes into account the fact that we do not solely perceive our world in terms of object shapes and spatial relations. We may also perceive our world via object action or possibilities. In other words one's perception of an object implies the action associated with it.[13] Gibson recognizes that the list of five separate senses is inadequate, preferring to refer to a 'haptic system' as a functional definition of touch which he defines as 'the sensibility of the individual to the world adjacent to his body by the use of his body' whereby 'men are literally in touch with their environment'.[14] This might relate very well to a First World War pilot flying his aeroplane for flying was a relatively new technology and, in essence, facilitated a new way of moving and being in the air. It provided a new environment which aviators had to learn how to be in. In interpreting the senses as active systems for perception, and thereby undermining dualisms between mind and body, Gibson focuses on how perception evolved to provide the means for animals or people to acquire information about and act accordingly within their environments.[15] As flying was a new way of moving, concepts of the cultural aspects of the passing of time, scale, and distance in relation to the pilot provide important analytical frameworks in seeking to discover how such concepts are experienced by the pilots of past flying technologies.[16]

Yet, as we will see, for a First World War pilot, the sense of touch in all its forms – haptics – is of critical importance, in fact paramount to his survival. Haptics pertains to the nature of, involving, or relating to the senses of touch, the perception of position and motion (proprioception), and other tactile and kinaesthetic sensations.[17]

Modern conflict archaeology addresses our most recent past in conflict but has not yet focused on man's relationship with an open-cockpit aeroplane and the activity and experience of flying in the First World War. I, therefore, adopt an approach based on an archaeology of the senses – particularly that of touch, or the haptic senses – in order to structure First World War aviators' descriptions of their sensory experiences whilst flying open-cockpit, and thereby to materialize aviators' experiences in terms of charting the beginning of the development of modern sensibilities in aviation. It was a new way of moving and Chapters 3 and 4 conceptualize and explore the haptic experiences of a First World War aviator in terms of spatial, physical, and environmental dimensions.

The First World War exposed the human body to conditions never before experienced. Newly trained pilots were forced to make sense of not only being in the air but also flying during conflict conditions in flimsy aeroplanes where imminent death was a constant possibility. These efforts 'capture[d] the central link between objects', in this case, aeroplanes, 'and bodily existence' as pilots learned to understand the sensorium in which they flew.[18] In focusing on First World War aviators' sensorial experiences of flying we learn that the sentient pilot 'body has a history and is as much a cultural phenomenon as it is a biological entity'.[19] Chapters 3 and 4 are illustrated throughout with quotes from First World War pilots which were gleaned from their diaries and published accounts. It is further interspersed with observations from my own flying experiences.

Fear and Anxiety

Whilst aviators recognized the full terror of aerial combat, First World War pilot Harold Balfour wrote that 'at the same time, [pilots] learnt in some way to cultivate a detachment of mind which enabled one, not to overcome fear but to separate oneself from it' so that the fight 'became impersonal: some secondary person did the right thing at the right moment; this secondary being took the initiative and would do some brave act or some clever manoeuvre; it was not oneself, for one's own real mind could watch this secondary being in operation'. It was not until the end of the fight, that 'one's personality displaced once more this secondary being and took charge of one's body' that the pilot became aware of the complete terror he had just experienced, a moment when his 'hands and feet shake and mouth go dry with fear'. Balfour often wondered if any of his comrades felt like this, but acknowledged that 'in those days such thoughts were still sacred and too intimate to bring to light'.[20]

Airmen were overwhelmed with anxiety, experiencing nightmares about going to their deaths in a spiralling aircraft that was on fire, being unable to escape their untimely death. Naturally fear and anxiety affected the bodies of the aviators as some of them were unable to control their senses. Fear takes its toll on the body, resulting in nervous conditions that the body is unable to prevent or control, John McGavock Grider writing, 'my nerves are all gone and . . . I've lived beyond my time already'.[21] Chapters 5, 6, and 7 reveal how airmen channelled their fears and anxieties when flying in combat. They explore how strategies for managing stress and hoped-for survival are reified in the form of rituals, omens, and objects. The chapters reveal how these strategies were materialized particularly in lucky mascots – inanimate objects vivified by the aviator's instinct to survive. As aviators created their social world, they introduced superstition and ritual as a means of restructuring their experiences in order to cope with new fears and anxieties. Of course, belief in such things during warfare is nothing new for the archaeological record is full of examples. In Roman times, for example, representations of male genitals in the form of copper alloy phallic amulets were carried by Roman soldiers in the first century AD as charms to protect against the evil eye and to encourage good luck and bestow male strength upon them.[22]

Whilst in Western empirical scientific thought it is not possible for objects to be magical by themselves, Alfred Gell, in *Art and Agency*, promotes the idea of the agency of things where '*persons* or "social agents" are, in certain contexts, substituted for by *art objects*'. For Gell an agent was one who 'causes events to happen' and 'whenever an event is believed to happen because of an intention lodged in the person or thing which initiates the causal sequence, that is an instance of agency'.[23] This idea is especially useful in my analysis of the agency of magic and folklore in lucky mascots because it is less what an art object represents than what it does within the social world of the aviators that has significance.

Often the owners of mascots do not regard their objects as being historically significant or having the capacity to help academic research understand the experiences of war. This book therefore strives to make visible and significant what has been invisible and regarded as insignificant for the last hundred years and thereby contribute a new material dimension to understanding the First World War.

Trench Art and Souvenirs

Trench art is defined as 'any item made by soldiers, [airmen], prisoners of war and civilians, from war materiel directly, or any other material, as long as it and they are associated temporally and/or spatially with armed conflict or its consequences'.[24] Trench art is arguably one of the most definitive kinds of conflict-related material culture. This book presents new insights into the relationship between people and objects both during and after the First World War. It seeks to unravel how objects, in the form of First World War air-related souvenirs and trench art, have become memory objects in today's world as tangible representations of past events.

Jay Winter in *Sites of Memory, Sites of Mourning* comments on the Cenotaph in Whitehall, London.[25] '[The] Cenotaph is a work of genius . . . because of its simplicity. It says so much because it says so little. It is a form on which anyone could inscribe his own thoughts, reveries, sadnesses.'[26] This can relate to the trench-art propeller grave markers described in Chapter 8. Nicholas Saunders invites us to consider trench art's 'capacity to link the temporal changes from war to peace in shapes and forms which appear the same but whose "social lives" and "cultural biographies" tell a diversity of stories'.[27] Some aeroplanes from the First World War have ended up as exhibits in a museum but, by applying a biographical approach, these can be considered as an object of multiple meanings as they move across space and time. With this in mind, my research is influenced by the idea of objects having biographies.

Arjun Appadurai introduced the idea that objects (he writes in terms of commodities and we can legitimately substitute other words such as aeroplane, lucky mascot, trench art, souvenir, etc.) have a story to tell because, like people, things have a 'social life'.[28] This approach is adopted as a powerful analytical tool throughout this book to investigate the relationship between aviators and the war materiel used to fabricate trench art not least because such '[o]bjects hold within themselves the worlds of their creators'.[29] In addition, since things cannot be fully comprehended at just one point in their lives, and because they change throughout their existence, anthropologist Igor Kopytoff's 'biographical' approach enables us to ask 'questions similar to those one asks about people', the 'cultural biography' of an object making 'salient what might otherwise remain obscure . . . [as things] are culturally redefined and put to use'.[30] Indeed, Kopytoff's work has influenced my treatment of trench art/souvenirs as I trace the events in the lives of pieces of aeroplane that have crashed that subsequently became part of people's lives in the past, are part of their lives in the present and might become part of their lives in the future.

Recognizing that remembering is a cultural process, Elizabeth Hallam and Jenny Hockey ask, 'how do the living maintain ongoing relationships with the dead in Western societies?'[31] This question is relevant for this book as I track the lives of propeller grave markers, as well as aviator-related trench art and souvenirs displayed in bereaved relatives' homes where some became important in the process of mourning and memorializing.

Since human experience is directly invested in material culture, modern conflict archaeology is a personal and experiential archaeology that 'excavates people's lives'.[32] In one sense, this book aims to provide a new and nuanced focus on modern conflict by offering another way of narrating the story in terms of focusing on the significant and non-obvious. In other words, there is more to the RFC and its aviators than the many aeroplanes exhibited in aviation museums alongside interpretation boards giving a host of technical details. How, we might ask instead, is a pilot's experience of flying in conflict conditions and his relationship with his aeroplane reified in material culture today?

Archaeology involves finding the means to give inanimate objects from the past a voice. Archaeologists amass and assess the evidence then interpret it. The following is my interpretation.

Chapter 3

Being in a First World War Aeroplane

The following is a somewhat unexpected quote with which to commence a chapter about fighting the First World War in the air but it is how Alan Bott described the end of an uneventful 3-hour patrol over enemy lines during freezing cold weather:

> Have you ever sucked bull's-eyes . . . If not, take it from me that the best time to try them is towards the end of a three-hour flight over enemy country. Five bull's eyes are then far more enjoyable than a five-course meal at the Grand Babylon Hotel. One of these striped vulgarities both soothes and warms me as we re-cross the trenches.[1]

It is a sentient piece of prose, and, although his patrol was uneventful, Bott would have been in a world of haptic activity as he concentrated hard on the job in hand, his body tense and alert.

First World War pilots experienced new ways of moving and being in a new environment. They were confronted with something never before encountered. Donal MacCarron's book about the life and letters of Denys Corbett Wilson, an Irish aviator who had been a Lieutenant in No. 3 Squadron, RFC, who died in 1915 wrote: '[t]ravelling in the comfort of today's aircraft, even in the sometimes cramped seats of economy class, cannot conceive of the Spartan conditions endured in the exposed cockpit of a Blériot. Perhaps this can be compared to cycling downhill at speed in to a strong icy wind?'[2] The 'nature' of the physical realities that challenged pilots, is an important consideration. Pilots often flew at temperatures below freezing point which caused their hands to go numb and 'since you could not stamp your feet, swing your arms, or . . . move at all, the numbness would spread to the . . . feet as well'.[3]

Competent flying would not necessarily save an aviator because the fragile biplanes, made from wood, metal, and linen, could break up at any time in airspace buffeted by strong crosswinds. In this space, vision was often restricted, even denied, as calculations of speed and distance were challenged by rain, hail, and snow in freezing temperatures. Canadian Roderick Ward Maclennan was commissioned as a Second Lieutenant in the RFC. He wrote about the intricacies and effects of the weather whilst flying:

> At 80 miles an hour rain drops cut into one's face like hailstones and the accumulation of rain and oil on the goggles makes it hard to see. This morning . . . my goggles [blew] . . . off . . . I was lucky to make a successful grab at them just as they were disappearing overboard.[4]

The natural agency of wind-driven cloud, rain, or snow caused occasions of 'drift' whereby a pilot had to steer in one direction in order to go in the other. Low-flying reconnaissance aeroplanes were well within the sights of ground-based German machine guns and rifles taking pot shots. Take-offs and landings were very risky, often doing so from the uneven surface of a field. In November 1914, for example, No. 3 Squadron's landing strip was fashioned from a beetroot field. It took a lot of physical effort to try to make this field suitable for landing and No. 3 Squadron was very fortunate in that a nearby Indian cavalry was in possession of a roller which it was willing to lend.[5]

There was the danger element that the engine could fail causing the aeroplane to crash if flown by an inexperienced pilot. Australian pilot Gordon Taylor joined the RFC (after being rejected by the Australian Flying Corps); he remembers his sense of timing was paramount when his Sopwith Scout suffered engine failure: 'It gave absolutely no warning, just stopped, leaving me there in appalling silence. It was my first experience of engine failure; in slightly less than one minute I knew I would be on the ground. Whether intact or not depended on what I did within the next three seconds.'[6]

Pilots constantly pushed boundaries experimenting with the tolerances of an aeroplane and honing their flying capabilities, to make new discoveries in flying technique, discoveries that could save their lives at a future date. RFC pilot Geoffrey Wall describes preparing to take off whilst sat in the observer's seat of an Avro aeroplane:

> Then, just as one felt that something was bound to go, the engine seemed to stop, and then some titanic power that I have never felt before – something 'outside' and uncontrollable – took hold of us, and we were climbing right into the dawn at 45 degrees. She climbed 'all out' for 2,000 feet then Harry flattened her out and 'stalled'. 'Stalling' is an operation which a year ago was looked on as an exceptionally sticky form of suicide. It consists of shutting off your engine and climbing until the machine loses way, and falls backwards. Just before she falls however, you put your nose downwards and bring her up again – see-sawing like this while she gradually settles down.[7]

Pilot and Aeroplane, a Haptic Engagement

The Haptic Space of an Aviator
My personal experience of flying in a Tiger Moth biplane informs that even getting into the plane requires good climbing skills and vestibular capability for there is a rhythm to it, like remembering dance steps.

The haptic space of an aviator was small, a fact that I noticed in the Tiger Moth, as my body immediately felt hemmed in as it practically filled the cockpit, my shoulders almost touching the sides and the instrument panel in front seemed very close to my face. Of course, the haptic space of different aeroplanes varied. For example, RFC pilot Captain Vernon Castle wrote in a letter of a captured German aircraft in Saint-Omer, France, observing that: 'The chief thing about their machines is that they are comfortable. Their seats are upholstered and roomy, and you can sit in them for hours and not get tired, while ours are small and make your back ache after half an hour's flight.'[8]

Flying is a world of verification. The pilot can physically 'feel' the aeroplane as though it is an integral part of himself, especially through the tactile points of bodily contact. First, he feels the aircraft through the pressure on his bottom. Second, when his hand makes tactile contact with the joystick his muscles engage to intentionally pull the stick lightly towards him, enabling the nose of the aeroplane to rise, pushing him further into his seat causing him to feel more pressure.[9] The joystick is sensitive and only a very slight touch is required so the pilot does not see it move, he can only feel it move.

A pilot uses his feet to apply pressure to two pedals – left and right – which control the aeroplane rudder, keeping it balanced and allowing him to control 'yaw'.[10] He accordingly feels the aircraft through his feet via the pressure of tactile contact and muscular exertion. Whilst the pilot has pedals on which he must place his feet, an observer must be careful where he puts his feet. Captain Paul Copeland Maltby recalls being on patrol at 7,000ft when his observer 'must have closed the air-flaps of [the] engine by fouling the wire with his foot. This gave . . . a forced landing in a field not far from the aerodrome which I misjudged . . . Spent the rest of the day replacing shock-absorber'.[11] An aviator needs to know how to use and not use his body in order to survive and learn.

Dressed to Fly
Conditions could be extreme when flying at altitude in open cockpits and aviators dressed accordingly. The First World War aviator wore specially designed clothes, such as a sheepskin flying jacket for warmth and goggles to protect the eyes. Such clothing contributed to the pilot's unique haptic experience, enabling him to fly and perform his duties, whether artillery observation, reconnaissance, aerial photography, bombing, or on fighter escort patrols. Sometimes, allocated RFC clothing was not suitable for the job at hand and it was common for aviators

to purchase additional equipment as their individuality and creativity came to the fore. Pilots were issued with regulation leather mittens which, 'having only the thumb separate and the fingers in a single heavy mitt to handle a Sopwith Scout was like trying to catch a feather with a cricket bat'.[12] Instead, pilot Gordon Taylor purchased gloves made from musquash, the soft leather fingers allowing for a more sensitive touch.[13] It is quite a remarkable parallel that, as aviators came to the Western Front from countries as far afield as Australia, Canada, New Zealand, and South Africa, some aviators wore gloves made from the imported fur of a North American rodent – and probably the first time that fur had been used at 10,000ft.

Aviators personally adapted their flying gear to feel more comfortable and, in a letter to his wife, Vernon Castle asked her to send him an old piece of fur. When flying, Castle experienced a cold draught blowing down his neck and thought it a good idea to sew a piece of fur onto the collar of his flying coat to prevent this.[14] Castle later wrote:

> The fur came today! . . . [it's] much too good for my flying coat. I am going to have it fixed on my British Warm. . . . I can buy a piece of cheap fur for my flying coat, because it will only get splashed with oil and rain, and would be a pity to waste good fur.[15]

To some extent, pilots could choose what they felt and, in this case, Vernon Castle did not wish to feel the touch of the wind.

Flying in an open-cockpit biplane I could feel the constraints and confines of the heavy leather and fur flying jacket pressing on my body and restricting my upper body movement, and, every time I moved I re-felt the touch of weight of the jacket. The touch of the fur collar on my neck made it tickle.

When Gordon Taylor first joined his squadron, he wore a warm woollen scarf under his flying jacket but the constant need to turn his head caused his neck to chafe so he substituted it for a silk scarf.[16]

Adapting to the Extremes of Flying

We take our skin for granted, until something nasty or uncomfortable happens to it. The extremes of temperatures on a hot sunny day were captured by Arthur Gould Lee who wrote of being very hot whilst sitting outside the office. Changing into flying kit had caused sweat to run down his skin and, on flying up towards the cold, he felt 'chillier and chillier, a most uncomfortable feeling, like being encased in an icy rubber sheet'.[17] Flying at different heights exposed airmen to a variety of temperatures, becoming colder the higher they flew.

The skin is the most sensitive of our organs and, covering the whole body, it provides a barrier between the body and the environment. As such, it presents as 'our first medium of communication, and our most efficient protector', registering sensations of pressure, temperature, and pain.[18] Flying in open cockpits meant that, at times, aviators were subjected to extreme cold. Hugh Granville White wrote that such cold was 'most painful, and inclined to induce tears. My fitter and rigger, like a couple of nannies, used to climb up and massage my legs whilst making sympathetic noises. They would eventually help me out of the aircraft.'[19]

Gordon Taylor wrote of being affected by facial frostbite whilst exposed to freezing conditions when flying at 10,000ft. Initially, he felt a burning pain all over his face that was akin to extreme sunburn. He wondered what caused it until somebody informed him it was frostbite.[20] Aircrew adapted and anti-cold precautions were designed to prevent the sensory assault of cold wind and frostbite. James McCudden, after feeling the physical effects of frostbite on his face, decided to wear the official leather Pattern flying mask that was issued for use.[21] Thus he managed to protect his face from the elements. Arthur Gould Lee also took precautions against frostbite by smearing whale grease all over his face, writing that 'the revolting aroma of the grease will haunt me all through patrol'.[22] Other measures were taken – Vaseline or engine grease was also applied to the face.

Flying at different heights exposed airmen to a diversity of temperatures. Gould Lee recalls descending from an 18,000ft, 2-hour patrol during which he felt extremely cold. But when flying at 3,000ft, it felt much warmer and he began to recover but 'the blood rushing through [his] half-frozen fingers gave [him] a stinging bout of pins and needles' making him very aware of his descent and of the varying thresholds that could be experienced at different altitudes.[23]

Sometimes the effects of elements such as snow and wind affected the body's tactile awareness. Wing Commander Eric Routh describes flying whilst severely hampered by the snow which invaded the cockpit from all angles and covered the windscreen. He had to lean out of the aeroplane to see where he was going. This caused his goggles to become covered in snow, and 'if I took them off snow got in my eyes and they watered . . . the only way I could see was to hold my hand in front of my face so that I could see downwards and occasionally slightly forward'.[24] In a similar manner, during my own Tiger Moth flight, I was aware of a very strange sensation of wind blowing up my nose which startled me and I am sure I could feel the cold wind in my mouth and taste it, the wind invading and, to some extent, alarming, my tactile awareness. Conversely, inner bodily substances, such as blood, courses through the body and, Gould Lee, shot in the calf whilst flying, '[c]ould feel the blood dripping down inside his flying suit'.[25] Hence tactile awareness can be a two-way experience as substances both enter and exit the body.

Cold wind is known to set sensitive teeth on edge. Denys Corbett Wilson became worried that his teeth would soon give him trouble when the wind 'touched them up'.[26] Many pilots experienced headaches due to the effects of flying at increasing heights. This caused Second Lieutenant Downing to take curative measures by writing home: 'Oh! By the way could you send me some asperines [*sic*] I have had pretty bad headaches just lately and think perhaps they would do me good'.[27] Man-made substances are, therefore, ingested to counter the adverse physical effects of being in the air through technological means. When descending from high altitudes, Hugh Granville White described how he suffered head and facial pains to 'the point where [he] could only descend in painful slow stages of a few hundred feet at a time, and it would take [him] up to 20 minutes on occasions to get down from 14,000–16,000 feet'.[28]

The sudden changes of altitude caused the ears to be painful. Following a flight in the observer's seat whilst the pilot demonstrated stunt manoeuvres, pilot Geoffrey Wall wrote in a letter:

> I felt all right but half an hour later I could hardly stand, and even now I feel a bit shaky. The sudden change in air pressure, I suppose. They take a lot of getting used to. Some pilots bleed at the nose and ears every time they go up.[29]

The sensations felt whilst flying could continue on the ground, the consequences of being able to move several thousand feet up and down. Indeed, when I flew the Tiger Moth, we came down to land fairly fast and the sudden change from low to high pressure blocked my ears for a while, making me temporarily deaf and somewhat disoriented.

The natural phenomena of clouds could be either friend or foe to the aviators. Very high clouds formed of ice crystals were an aviator's enemy for they provided 'a light background, against which aeroplanes are boldly silhouetted, to the greatest advantage of the anti-aircraft gunners'.[30] Conversely, the friendly clouds found several thousands of feet lower and formed of water vapour were useful if a pilot was flying above them for they helped him to dodge German anti-aircraft fire and 'when numerous enough to make attempts at observation ineffective, they perform an even greater service for him – that of arranging for a day's holiday'.[31] Flying inside the clouds is risky for the pilot's vision is restricted to not much more than 3ft beyond the wing tips of the aeroplane, 'nothing is to be seen but the aeroplane, nothing is to be heard but the droning hum of the engine, which seems louder than ever amid the isolation'.[32] Flying inside clouds, therefore, magnifies a very peculiar set of sensorial experiences.

Pilots frequently flew amongst the clouds in order to hide from German aeroplanes to avoid being the target of attack, so clouds in this sense were a natural phenomenon culturally reconfigured as 'camouflage' that pilots had to learn to use to their advantage. Since vision was reduced, it was necessary for the pilot to steer by compass without the aid of the sun or the sight of a landmark to guide him. The fighter pilot Cecil Lewis relates that 'it requires courage for a pilot to trust his instruments. He feels the aircraft is slipping this way or that, it is turning, stalling, diving. But he knows he must suppress his own instincts and keep everything straight and steady.'[33]

In a similar manner, air was culturally reconfigured to be used as a fire extinguisher whilst flying. During an interview, First World War pilot John Davies was asked what happened if his aeroplane caught fire whilst flying. He answered, 'the only way to avoid fire in the air was to sideslip and perhaps put the fire out – if you are going forward the flames come back at you but if you sideslip you can send them up that way and put the fire out'.[34] To sideslip, the pilot had to bank in one direction using the ailerons and the rudder in the opposite direction simultaneously. This caused the aeroplane to slip sideways left or right of the main longitudinal direction of travel causing an apparent wind on the face opposite to the direction of slip.[35]

Pilot–Aeroplane Relationship

Learning to fly was not easy and RFC trainees felt unfamiliar and awkward in their initial interactions with an aeroplane. Whilst undertaking training at Hendon Aerodrome, North London, Frederick Ortweiler speculated whether he could control the aircraft if it suddenly moved sideways or forward. He answered his own uncertainty with the positive comment, 'that feeling will no doubt soon come' as his body entered into a malleable relationship with his aircraft.[36] Ortweiler found it difficult to tell if his aircraft was horizontal longitudinally and laterally. At times, when he thought the aeroplane was 'right', his instructor corrected it because Ortweiler had not yet developed his flying instinct in terms of skill and experience. On this occasion: '[Ortweiler] found afterwards that it was the old bus' fault; to fly her straight it was necessary to keep on a bit of right rudder and as I did not know it, and kept the rudder-bar straight, she naturally did not fly right.'[37]

In an archived taped interview held at the Imperial War Museum, James Gascoyne recalls his training days at Thetford in 1917. He relates how his flight instructor informed him 'how clumsy [he] was, too heavy footed [and] too heavy handed'.[38] Nervous pupils often clutched 'the joystick so firmly that the instructor would have difficulty using the dual controls to correct the error being made'.[39]

From my own experience, the first time I apprehensively took control of the Tiger Moth, flying at 1,000ft, judging by the pilot's comments to me over the intercom – he called me a 'hooligan' – I was too heavy handed in that I gripped the joystick tightly and the pilot had to caution me to be 'nice and gentle' because he was unable to move the controls.

Even when a pilot obtained his brevets (flying wings), he still had to learn how to fly different aeroplanes in terms of understanding their handling capabilities and feeling their tolerances; some aeroplanes, like the RE8 aircraft, felt particularly heavy and cumbersome.[40] However, according to Arthur Gould Lee, the Sopwith Pup was another story for it 'was a dream to fly, so light on the control, so effortless to handle, so sweet and amenable, and so eagerly manoeuvrable that you found yourself doing every kind of stunt without a thought – loops, sideslip landings, tail slides, rolls, spins'.[41]

Flying a captured German Albatros aeroplane, Gordon Taylor learned much about the opposition's air power.[42] As the Albatros gathered speed to take off, it had to 'run quite a distance before it showed any inclination to leave the ground' following which Taylor 'could feel the wheels rattling light upon the surface of the stubble field'. Taylor then applied 'a little back pressure on the stick' (backward movement to raise the nose) to become airborne.[43] The pilot's sense of bodily movement (kinaesthesia) is invoked here as he tenses his muscles from within to hold the machine in a steady climb to 1,000ft.[44] He applied the controls to a left-hand turn. Whilst the aircraft was flying at a lateral angle, Taylor felt 'it was quite light'. When he applied more pressure on the stick to steepen the turn and tried to pull the machine round with the elevator (and by applying his foot to the rudder pedal to maintain airspeed), 'it seemed very heavy, putting up a resistance to the turn'.[45] Pulling back harder on the stick increases the rate of turn of an aeroplane, but becomes physically harder to do so that the pilot's arms and body are taut with strain as he tenses his muscles to hold and balance the aircraft. Taylor could see immediately why the Albatros pilots avoided 'the close duelling turns' for it was the aeroplane that was most manoeuvrable and quickest in the turn that was most likely to win in combat. The feel of the aircraft helped him 'see' in terms of accumulating knowledge of the tolerances of an enemy aircraft which would help him with haptic tactics when he encountered an Albatros on future occasions.

Whilst novice pilots could be clumsy and heavy handed, experienced pilots could 'feel' a cumbersome and heavy aeroplane. Similarly, pilots could 'feel' a well-designed aircraft, particularly one that was not susceptible to every bump experienced in the air and on the ground. As Maclennan noted about his Avro trainer, it was:[46]

> . . . so well designed that bumps need hardly be considered by the pilot. They chuck his machine about and would do this to any bus

made but an Avro corrects these herself and the pilot does not have to be continually waggling the stick about as he does on a BE2b.[47]

The felt tolerances of an aeroplane were culturally important to aviators of the RFC but were not immediately apparent – they came with experience and were bodily ways of knowing in terms of representing a 'culturally constructed sensorium'.[48] First World War aviators saw the boundaries between man and machine dissolve. The sentient pilot body as a culturally constructed entity was culturally transformed and humans and machines became entangled.[49]

Haptic Activities

The pilot had a purpose beyond flying his aeroplane – such as reconnaissance and taking aerial photographs and shooting at the enemy – all of which required his sense of touch in haptic activities. For example, in some aeroplanes, when attacked from behind, the pilot had to stand in his seat, hold the joystick between his knees – relying on his vestibular sense to maintain his balance and steady the machine in the air – whilst simultaneously holding his gun steady in order to fire backwards over the top of the aircraft.[50] Such balance enabled him to keep his hand steady for long enough to allow him to squeeze the trigger, causing death and destruction through the touch of a finger – the touch of conflict.

Whilst training as an observer at the Aerial School of Gunnery, in 1916, Second Lieutenant Downing wrote in a letter:

> Today I have been up twice and feel quite at home in an old bus now, although I have not quite got used to the standing up stunt, . . . that is, you are perched right out in front of the machine in a small nascelle about a foot high, and whilst anything from a thousand feet high, stand up and fire at targets, balloons etc, with a machine gun, whilst the old machine you are in, is perhaps tearing to earth, at about 90mph.
>
> I expect you think that this is rather far-fetched, but . . . it is not, . . . after the first few times, you take no notice . . . as you cannot fall out, the pressure of the wind prevents it, but I must admit to commence with, it gives you a nasty feeling in the tummy.[51] (see Figure 3)

The airmen of the RFC took aerial photographs to map enemy positions for counter-battery fire. In a letter to his wife, dated 1 July 1916, referring to oblique photographs taken at an angle, Vernon Castle wrote:[52]

Figure 3. *An observer demonstrating the precarious stance required to use the rear-facing Lewis gun, Sainte-Marie-Cappel, France, 1918.* (© IWM (Q69650))

> This photography is the worst job one can get because [the photos] have to be taken very low and one is well in range. I had my plane hit three times with pieces of shell, and the concussion you get makes you think the machine is blown in half . . . I was sick with fright.[53]

Castle flew patrols during the Battle of the Somme taking many aerial photographs, an activity that, as well as connecting with the camera, meant that the pilot had to multi-task whilst engaging with his aeroplane. Since the camera was fixed to the aircraft, the pilot had to manoeuvre his aeroplane to point the camera at the required spot to be photographed. As he looked down through two cross-wire sights, when the target was in focus, he had to simultaneously operate a plate camera to take the aerial photographs. This process of hand-and-eye coordination required continuous attention to the camera sights and a disregard of enemy aircraft, such disregard causing Captain Herman Lloyd Tracy to feel his 'hair literally stand up'. Tracy had to take twenty-four plates and it 'seemed to take 24 hours to expose them all with A [Archie (anti-aircraft shells)] and EA [enemy aeroplanes] doing their bit in the neighbourhood'.[54]

The technology of aerial photography extended the reach of the pilot who did not want to remain under fire but had to complete his task all the while resisting his natural urge to flee from danger as his sense of duty took hold. His urge to flee was restrained and superseded by other haptic senses for, as he held his breath in concentration, he felt his mouth go dry and, as he tensed his muscles until they ached, he tried to concentrate on the haptic activity in hand.

An aviator made notes of his observations and sometimes sketched maps in flight but, with such little space to achieve this, his body was haptically modified by attaching a knee desk to his upper leg in order that his duties could be fulfilled efficiently.

It could be awkward writing whilst flying in the air and, sometimes, an aviator avoided touching the sides of his aircraft so as not to feel the vibration, as Alan Bott elaborates:

> Passing a few small woods, we arrived without interruption over the railway junction of Boislens. With arms free of the machine to avoid unnecessary vibration, the observers trained their glasses on the station and estimated the amount of rolling stock. A close search of the railway arteries only revealed one train. I grabbed pencil and notebook and wrote: 'Boislens, 3.5 P.M. 6 R.S., 1 train going SW'.[55]

Here, haptic verification is put to one side in favour of a haptic activity as aviators were able to choose their haptic experience in order to accomplish the task in hand.

Aviators could feel movement through the air such as enemy fire, for '[t]ouch may not contact a distant movement in the environment directly, but feel the vibration generated in materials in contact, or reach of, the body' or the aeroplane.[56] James McCudden remembered flying an aircraft whilst directing the fire of an Allied 15in Howitzer gun noting '[t]he bursts of their 15-inch shells were enormous, and even at 6,000 feet we would feel in the machine slight concussion after the shells burst'.[57] Similarly, in April 1917, whilst flying over Arras, France, when all the guns on both sides in the district were firing, pilot Lieutenant Charles Smart recalled '[t]he whole ground, particularly on the enemies side, was simply seething with bursting shells . . . [and] [t]he air was just stiff with flying shells and we got no end of bumps from them as they passed under and over us', bringing the touch of the war on the ground a bit too close for comfort in the air world, but linking the two sensorial zones as up and down merged.[58]

Chapter 4

Reshaping the Aviator's Body and Mind

Re-configuring the Human Body

First World War open-cockpit biplanes extended the human capacity for movement. Many pilots compared flying open-cockpit aeroplanes to riding a horse:

> The [Sopwith] Pup . . . was a joy to fly, with smooth and willing engine, and very sensitive response to the controls, just like a spirited horse, eager to the slightest touch of rein and knee. . . . you feel as though you're controlling a living thing, as though the two of you are one creature gambolling in the air.[1]

Many pilots died during the First World War due to inexperience and having insufficient flying hours. Constant flying practice and, therefore, mounting experience of flying the aeroplane and getting to know its peculiarities meant that the pilots' bodies were haptically re-configured as they learned to instinctively feel and handle their aircraft with confidence: '[t]he best pilots are "part" of their machines and we were always encouraged to be so at home with our aircraft that nothing could surprise us. Our reactions in an emergency would be "second nature", instinctive, *as if the aeroplane was an extension of our very self*.'[2]

When firing a gun on the ground, a marksman positions his body in a suitable stance, raises his arm, aims, and fires. However, in the air the aeroplane substitutes for the body as the pilot aims the aircraft. As Gould Lee observes, '[y]ou don't aim the [Vickers] gun, that's fixed in the line of flight, you aim the aeroplane with joystick and rudder'.[3]

Learning to fly is not a straightforward matter because an expert flyer of the Sopwith Camel was not immediately proficient in flying a Bristol Fighter. A pilot has to 'know' his machine in terms of its peculiarities and the best way to handle it. He must also know how his aeroplane will react in certain circumstances and how to act in response.

Re-configuring the Senses

Aviators' senses were re-configured and culturally constructed as they learned to engage with a new way of moving. It is claimed that vision has been prioritized over other senses in the Western world.[4] But sometimes seeing in our own recent historical world is not a straightforward concept for it is a matter of knowing *how* to look and this is particularly relevant when flying.

Sight is an active ability that deploys not just the eyes but other parts of the body as muscles are engaged that turn the head or focus the eyes. The pilot must, at all times, maintain a high visual awareness of the environment outside the cockpit. He must relate the attitude (or nose position) of the aeroplane to the natural horizon and hold the aircraft on an even keel, or, indeed, in any position, by reference to the horizon.[5] A pilot must also check his passage over ground, look out for other aircraft, and avoid flying into clouds. Flying an aeroplane depends on a number of perceptual abilities that are necessary to gauge depth, distance, and motion. The spatial character of a pilot's visual world is given not by the aeroplane but by the background to the aircraft for the pilot's space is 'determined by the ground and the horizon, not by the air through which he flies'.[6]

As a pilot learns body techniques regarding eye movements when he visually scans his aerial environment, it is this vital practice that enables him to 'see accurately a continuous visual world in which he himself moves with precision'.[7] The pickup of information through head turning, Gibson calls *visual kinesthesis*.[8]

Cecil Lewis explains:

> ... the fighting pilot's eyes are not on the ground, but roving endlessly through the lower and higher reaches of the sky, peering anxiously through fur-goggles to spot those black slow-moving specks against land or cloud which mean full throttle, tense muscles, held breath, and the headlong plunge with screaming wires – a Hun in the sights, and the tracers flashing.[9]

It was quite common for men with excellent sight on the ground to appear blind at times when flying through the atmosphere because an inexperienced pilot 'had to give most of his attention to the leader, watching closely for signals; he therefore could not be expected to see as much as one whose eyes were attuned to distance and whose whole attention could be given to finding the enemy'.[10] But even finding the enemy was not a straightforward process for haptic tactics had to be deployed to see them. For example, Rothesay Stuart Wortley, a RFC Flying Officer, wrote about new flying recruits in his diary:

> The Flight Commander has experience: he can see a great deal more than the tyro;[11] and he knows where to look. If he does not dive on a Hun . . . a few thousand feet below him, it is because he recognises in that Hun a bait, and at once looks upward to perceive a formation of enemy scouts waiting to swoop in their turn on his tail.[12]

In looking up, the Flight Commander is not just using his sight but is engaging his neck muscles to turn and focus his eyes. Flying changes how you see and the sense of sight has a tactile dimension for it involves eye movement and head turning. For the aviator vision is not an objectifying sense but should be understood in terms of its interrelationship with other senses. Flying an aeroplane involves both skilled vision and skilled bodily movement. A pilot's trained eyes and haptic responses create a sentient technology of the pilot body because operational sight is engaged in the form of visual kinesthesis as a pilot's eyes become attuned to distance by scanning his aerial environment. Such skilled vision, or re-configured means of seeing, has evidently re-shaped human consciousness as it engages with new technologies.

The reconnaissance undertaken by the RFC was crucial in the lead-up to the Battle of the Somme in 1916.[13] Lieutenant A.J. Evans, of No. 3 Squadron, wrote about recognizing features in the landscape from aerial photographs taken just a few days before the Battle of the Somme commenced:

> Only an expert observer would know that the thin straight line was a light railway; that the white lines were paths made by the ration parties and reliefs following the dead ground when they came up at night; that the almost invisible line was a sunken pipe line for bringing water to the trenches, and that the shading which crept and thickened along the German reserve trenches showed that the German working parties were active at night if invisible in the day time. For the shading spelt barbed wire.[14] (See Figures 4 and 5 for an example of an aerial photo and its accompanying interpretive sketch)

Pilots took several vertical aerial photographs of particular areas with a 60 per cent overlap that could be viewed together through a stereoscope (see Figure 6) to bring forth the perception of depth and, therefore, useful in intelligence derived from aerial photographs.[15] Such an assisted means of seeing culturally enhanced the illusion of depth and interpretation of what was seen.

The design limitations of some First World War aircraft denied vision to pilots. Indeed, during my own flight I could not see out to the front of the plane because the wings blocked my vision. I could see to the right and left though the

32   The Archaeology of the Royal Flying Corps

Figure 4. *An aerial photograph. Area: River Ancre to River Somme. La Bassée Canal to River Scarpe.* (© IWM (LBY EPH 1009))

wings restricted my vision. In the air, blind spots caused by design forced the pilot to manoeuvre his aircraft by flying at an angle for an improved view. This required that the pilot understand the flying abilities of his aeroplane in order that he could overcome design limitations. He would then be able to observe in all directions without obstruction. Whilst on patrol in cold weather, Gould Lee remembers 'tipping the machine laterally and swerving lightly, to uncover the blind spots'.[16]

During the First World War, in the absence of night training and luminous dials on instruments, neither aeroplanes nor pilots were equipped to fly in the dark. Sholto Douglas recalls being in France and he 'had on occasions landed . . . as it was getting dark, but . . . could not claim that [he] had any real experience of flying at night'. Whilst Flight Commander at a flying school in England, Douglas purposely tried more elaborate night flying, remembering he 'flew for a while after nightfall in a BE2c, completing what was then quite a venture by landing

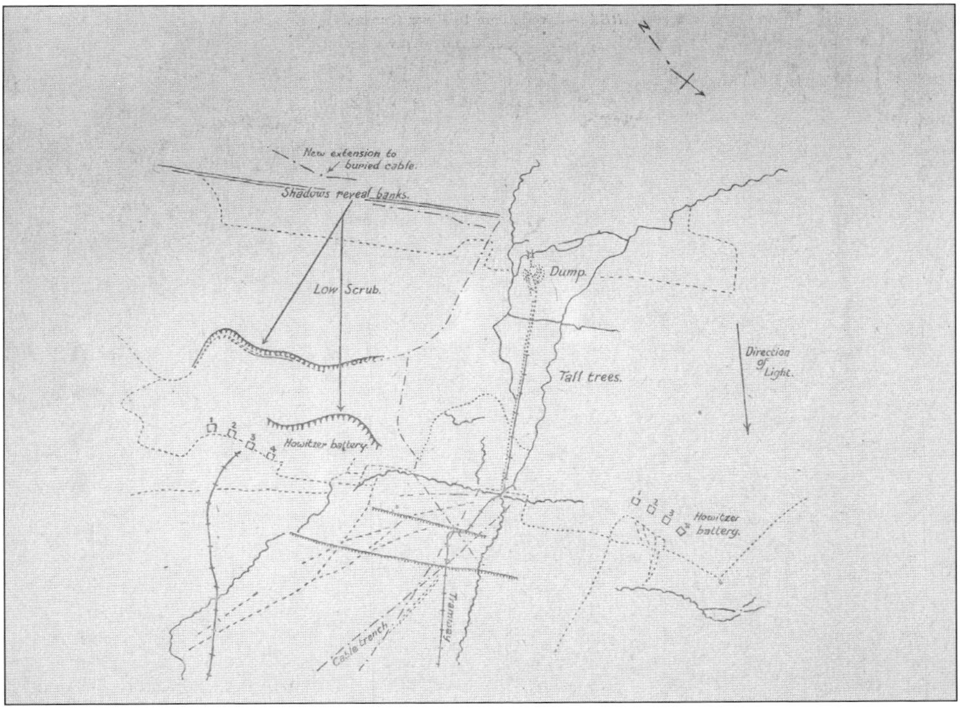

Reshaping the Aviator's Body and Mind   33

Figure 5. *An interpretative sketch of the aerial photograph seen in Figure 4.* (© IWM (LBY EPH 1009))

Figure 6. *A stereoscopic viewer and simple eye piece.*
(© IWM (LBY EPH 1009))

with the help of flares. "Easier than expected. Could see sea and lights, but not wood or roads", [he] recorded in [his] flight log book'.[17]

Pilots managed to overcome technological deficiencies and they did so by 'feel and instinct'.[18] Cecil Lewis recalls raiding the aerodrome stores for hand torches to fly at night because German aeroplanes were approaching the Thames estuary. He remembers that somebody rigged up a line of flares made from paraffin-soaked cotton waste burning in a bucket to enable him to take off. The smoky smell filled his cockpit, assaulting his nostrils as it dominated his haptic awareness. He always associated that smell with his first night flight.[19] This was because '[m]emory as a distinct meta-sense transports, bridges and crosses all the other senses'.[20] As pilots learned to fly at night, their haptic senses became ever more refined as the pilot body became tense and alert to compensate for reduced vision. A pilot became, for example, ultra-sensitive to each vibration of his aeroplane's engine. On the night of Lewis' first night flight, the moon shone bright, aiding his vision and he could hear his engine revolutions and feel his air speed as his haptic senses were heightened to compensate for his reduced vision.[21]

Archibald Yuille recalls flying on a night patrol, whereby:

> . . . you were just there, up by yourself, in the dark, for two hours. . . . you'd come down absolutely hoarse because one of the things one did was to sing. We used to sing quite unconsciously . . . Well, it's lonely; two hours up there in the darkness seeing nothing. It's an extraordinary effect and not everybody has the mentality to do that.[22]

Many airmen wrote of singing whilst flying to relieve the boredom. The RFC had a repertoire of songs and rhymes, often sung to the music of an already existing and well-known tune with a repetitive chorus. Some of their rhymes 'engaged the sense of touch through the tactile and kinaesthetic dimensions of speech'.[23] The words of tongue-twisters enabled them to feel the words through their mouths, and the following is an example of alliteration being employed:

> Heavy handed Hans flies Halberstadters,
> In handy, Halberstadters for a flight our Hans does start;
> . . .
> See how heavy-handed Hans ham-handles handy Halberstadts![24]

Sound was especially important to First World War pilots. Apart from the distinctive noise of different aero engines, singing was popular binding men together in their respective squadron messes, often with dark humour, as in this chorus from 'The Dying Aviator':

> Take the cylinder out of my kidneys,
> The connecting rod out of my brain,
> The cam box from under my backbone,
> And assemble the engine again.²⁵

As fighter pilot Arthur Gould Lee recalls, such:

> . . . dirge-like doggerels were a mock-heroic rejection of fear, a maudlin scoffing at mortality, a reduction of gory extinction to the level of nursery rhymes, yet they were sung as lustily by veterans who had seen sudden death, and escaped by inches, as they were by novices . . . to whom a violent end by bullets was still entirely an abstraction.²⁶

New Haptic Thresholds

Flying up to 20,000ft was a new feat of endurance during the First World War. As pilots of the RFC pushed their aircraft and their bodies to limits unimaginable at the outbreak of the war, aviators experienced new corporeal feelings, such as the effects of centrifugal force and breathing difficulties. Novice pilot Geoffrey Wall wrote in a letter home:

> I glanced at the speed indicator – 65, yet no sensation of speed. I seemed to be standing still . . . It was about time I turned. Over went the joystick, and down went one wing tip; I trod on the rudder at the same time – an alarming sensation – but of course this was centrifugal force, I had read about it.²⁷

It could take 15 minutes to climb to 10,000ft, although it felt much longer, and up to 30 minutes to climb to 15,000ft because the higher the aeroplane went, the slower it became.²⁸ Air is less dense at altitude so the propeller and engine become less effective as there is less oxygen to burn. Supercharged engines had not yet been invented and these would have overcome the altitude problem in that they could suck in more air per unit of petrol.

When learning to fly, Gordon Taylor remembers taking a test to prove he could reach a height of 6,000ft. He had only ever flown at 2,000ft and was uncertain what the effects on his body at such a great height would be. He gradually flew to heights of 5,000ft which caused breathing difficulties, whilst heights of 5,400ft made him feel dizzy. He gradually grew accustomed to ever increasing heights until, some three months later, he was easily flying at 17,000ft.²⁹

Critical signs of being alive include a beating heart and a breathing body but these occur in the background of our bodily awareness, only coming to our attention when something out of the ordinary occurs, such as the effects on the body of flying at high altitudes. Gould Lee was aware of the effects of flying at 15,000ft for he could feel his heart thumping and he noticed that he was breathing in long open-mouthed gasps to compensate for the lack of oxygen.[30]

It was only through men being prepared to exercise their sense of risk and adventure, to see how high they could fly in the aircraft of the day that fuelled technological innovation to overcome thresholds as pilots adapted to their environment and re-configured their sensibilities. Of course, such thresholds are not without limits. To achieve ever higher altitudes, the sentient pilot body was further adapted by using oxygen masks to facilitate breathing, thus making it an 'artefact *in extremis*'.[31]

The noise of the aircraft's engine confirmed to the pilot that the aircraft was performing correctly, 'the roar of the motor feel[ing] like the very lifeblood', the pilot seeking the human traits of being alive in his machine.[32] A pilot would instantly be alerted to occasions when the engine cut out which could signify trouble for an 'airman is accustomed to the full roar of his engine, and it never distracts his attention, any more than the noise of a waterfall distracts those who live near it. But if the roar becomes non-continuous and irregular he is acutely conscious of the sound'.[33] That is unless it had been purposely cut to promote a safe landing for these early flying machines glided into land: 'When the engine is shut off and the nose of the machine pointed towards the earth in order to come down, the beginner usually has a horrible sinking feeling about the stomach. This sensation entirely disappears as one does more and more flying.'[34]

The pilot becomes familiar with the new sensations of stretched bodily tolerances and, gliding back to earth at '70 miles an hour with the engine off, without the pilot's hands touching any of the controls', could result in 'probably the most pleasing sensation of any'.[35]

As the human body had to adjust to flying high, allowances had to be made for descending to allow it time to adjust and acclimatize to the higher air pressure and temperatures. Personal experience of coming in to land was that the rapid reduction in height caused my ears to become blocked temporarily. The physical effects of flying continued on land, thereby joining the two physical and sensorial realms. Some pilots discovered a way to avoid hearing difficulties and resorted to chewing gum or sucking boiled sweets, such as the already mentioned bull's eyes.

Communication

Whilst the haptic senses are a means of bringing physical phenomena to our attention, they also bring forth cultural values, for example, in terms of sensory communication, as aviators had to develop ways of communicating with each other whilst in the air.

At flight training school, Frederick Ortweiler sat in the front of a two-seater aeroplane and could feel the instructor tap him on the back to signal that he wanted Ortweiler to take control and fly the plane.[36] This was a pre-agreed form of communication between the trainee pilot and the flight instructor. Similarly, a tap on the right or left shoulder indicated a right- or left-hand turn; a tap on the top of the head meant to put the nose down to descent; and a tap on the back of the neck meant pull the control column back and climb.[37] Ortweiler could not see his instructor and, if his instructor spoke to him whilst flying, he would not be able to hear him. Since his senses of vision and hearing were denied, touch became the mode of communication. Hence the relationship between the instructor and the trainee pilot was structured by their mutual sense of touch as one touches and the other is touched.

In two-seater aeroplanes, the pilot sitting in front of the observer could not hear the other speak but the innovative airmen found ways round this. At first they wrote each other messages or shut down the engine. Such actions however used up too much time. Then there was 'an experiment with a speaking-tube similar to those through which a waiter in a Soho restaurant demands [food] from an underground kitchen' but the noise of the engine again defeated this innovation. Bott describes how eventually a forward-thinking pilot fitted a mouthpiece and earpiece to a length of tubing, which solved the problem.[38]

Aircraft and pilots' bodies also merged when flying in formation, as the flight leader used his aeroplane to communicate to the other pilots when they should turn in unison. He had to control the aeroplane to make pilot-coordinated gesticulatory movements to mimic culturally recognized signals and gestures. During summer 1917, the basic rules of flying in formation began to be worked out as pilots had to negotiate their haptic world with precision to avoid contact with another aeroplane within the formation. This was not easy, for if the:

> ... engine develops a sudden increase of revolutions, and the pilot finds himself overhauling the craft in front; he throttles back and finds himself being overhauled by the craft behind; a slight deviation from the course and the craft all around seem to be swinging sideways or upwards. Not till a pilot can fly his bus unconsciously does he keep place without repeated reference to the throttle and instrument board.[39]

In addition, there was no radio telephone and successful formation flying was achieved through the use of pre-agreed signals. Such signals could be in the form of physical gestures made by the pilot, controlling the aircraft in a particular manner, or by firing coloured Verey lights, different colours conveying varying messages of manoeuvre intent.[40] The use of coloured Verey lights characterizes flying in terms of communication and colour is used to cause a sense of movement as the pursuing aviators comply with the colour code to perform the correct haptic response required to remain in formation. One aviator remembered flying in a formation of six aircraft in the form of a very close-knit triangle using a specific set of agreed signals to communicate with the pilots flying the other aeroplanes:

> If [N] is going to turn sharp, he drops his wing on that side. . . . to call our attention to something he shakes both wings. If it's a Hun, he shakes his wings and points and fires his guns. If he means 'yes' he bobs his nose up and down . . . if he means 'no' he shakes his wings. . . . If he wants us to follow him out of a fight, he fires a white light.[41]

It was vital that a scout patrol maintained a strong formation tightly focused and responsive to the movements of its leader who was responsible for manoeuvring the flight; when the leader decided to turn, all the other pilots in the formation had to manoeuvre their aeroplanes accordingly, for example:

> . . . a turn to the right would be signalled by rocking the machine from side to side and then dropping a wing down to the right and commencing the turn. The pilot on the right of the leader would slow their engines and pull their machines up, slowing them as much as possible, while the leader would fly round in a normal manner; those on the left who had to complete the outer and greater circle would put their noses down and go as fast as possible to catch up; thus would a turn be made, and when all were on an even keel after the turn each pilot would close up to his original distance from his next man. Such a manoeuvre came easily after practice but, to an inexperienced pilot, it was extremely difficult.[42]

In effect, the pilot controls the aeroplane to make pilot-coordinated movements to mimic culturally recognized signals and gestures. In this manner, the aircraft becomes an extension of the human body and is used to communicate meanings and intentions in the air as humans and non-humans seemingly became entangled.

Aerial reconnaissance photographs were studied for potential targets. RFC pilot John Davies explains how a further means of communication was developed between the aircraft in the air and artillery batteries on the ground so that the aviators could successfully direct the ranging of the guns.[43] This added another dimension to the war on the ground. In a curious twist of the senses, aviators became the eyes of the army, enabling those manning artillery on the ground to 'see' beyond their immediate horizon and wage war beyond the infantry's battlefield and thereby extending the scale and nature of conflict landscape. As aviators sometimes operated wirelesses in the air, RFC wireless operators were attached to gun batteries on the ground to enable aviators to communicate information to the batteries.[44] But the wireless was not two-way and the aviators could not receive messages.

Davies remembers working with the artillery and directing:

> . . . where their shoots were falling . . . The Battery put out an 'L' [in cloth strips] to say they were firing. You picked that up and you went over and watched where their shots were falling . . . the aerial photographs were ringed . . . A, B, C, and D in which 12 o'clock was the head of the ring, so you sent down the number of the ring and the time 1, 2, 3, so they knew exactly where their shots were falling.[45]

Observers soon grew accustomed to sending Morse code whilst in a moving aeroplane. Observers were trained in Morse code to '"buzz" at sixteen words per minute. This led to their working at about twelve words per minute in the air' giving an aura of tactility to speech as hands and fingers substituted for mouths and invisible signals were sent through the invisible air via the tactile pressure exerted by the fingertips.[46] The use of wireless technology hitherto 'extends the reach of the body and can give . . . a sense of experiencing a world apart from the body' but also, in effect, of unifying both worlds.[47] Evidently both the wireless operator and the aviator became 'distributed persons' as they became instrumental in causing events to happen in areas nowhere near their bodies.[48]

Altering Cultural Perceptions of Time and Space

Flying afforded a new way of moving which altered aviators' cultural perception of time, space, speed, and distance. For example, as lived experience, flying in dangerous conditions distorted an aviator's sense of time. My own experience of flying at 1,000ft certainly resonated with this for the traffic below appeared to be moving slowly on the roads; perception of speed seemed to change when looking down from above and I felt we were flying in slow motion.

Sometimes our relationships with moving objects can be disorienting. For instance, 'in an aeroplane you have very little sensation of speed, except when near the ground'.[49] It is 'the speed indicator, mounted on the instrument board in front of his knees, alone lets [the pilot] know the difference between 40 and 80 miles'.[50] Thus the pilot is not conscious of those speeds as velocity at height cannot be sensed, only technologically informed, the speed indicator providing information that the senses cannot perceive to distinguish illusion from reality. Evidently, flying an aeroplane during the First World War defined the relationship between humans and technology as technology became a substitute for a pilot's sense of knowing and verification.

On occasion, strong contrary winds affected the forward motion of the aeroplane through the air. Any aircraft returning from a flight over enemy lines normally had the prevailing wind against it which slowed it down. But when the wind was strong, Second Lieutenant Geoffrey Mayne Hopkins informs us that the ground speed was significantly reduced presenting aviators as 'sitting birds for the anti-aircraft guns'. On trying to land at the aerodrome, Hopkins remembers situations when the wind speed was greater than the landing speed and the engine had to be switched on because the 'aeroplane was flying backwards, relative to the ground'.[51] The verdict of the case of nature versus technology is a confusion of the senses for nothing is more disorientating for a pilot than to think he is moving forward when, in fact, he is moving backwards.

The natural agency of wind-driven cloud, rain, snow, and sleet affected movement too and Corbett Wilson describes flying a reconnaissance mission whilst it was snowing: 'There was a most 'orrible drift on, and we took an awful long time to get to Armentieres. . . . Coming home I had to steer due north to get West [an example of "drift"].'[52]

On the Western Front, aeroplanes and their aviators were targets for machine guns and high explosives. Pilots soon learned to recognize the strange noise of anti-aircraft shells (Archie) for a burst nearby 'sounds like a giant clapping his hands and it has a sort of metallic click'.[53] Though it was known that the bursts you could hear would not harm you, it did alert the pilot that the gun battery had him within range and the next one would be closer.[54] This sonic news triggered his perceptual haptic responses to manoeuvre the aeroplane in a zig-zag pattern to make it difficult for a German gunner to keep him within range and causing him to fire where the pilot should have been had he not taken evasive action. It is calculated that 'the best thing to do is to change your course twenty degrees every twelve seconds. That gives you time to get out of the way of the one that's coming up at you that moment and doesn't give the gunners time to get your deflection for the next shot'.[55] Manoeuvring in this way was like a performance with timed movements and rhythms; it was like dancing in the air. It was pilot skill and calculation in terms of timing and moving through the air that avoided being in the air space where a German gunner calculated he would be. Lewis calculated that he could fly a distance of 400yd between the time an anti-aircraft shell was fired and the moment it burst. The pilots learned that the gun bursts to be avoided at all costs could not be heard, only seen, as they appeared 'silently like puff balls in the sky'.[56]

The German gunner on the ground and the pilot in the air were each trying to outguess and outmanoeuvre the other by playing with perceptions of time, space, and distance. This novel situation revolutionized human experiences of, and adaptation to, this new technologically created sensorial realm.

The Aldis collimation sight was used to estimate the distance to the target to inform the pilot or observer when a shot could be taken.[57] Some pilots did not like them though and had them removed from their aeroplanes. It was removed from William Barker's Sopwith Camel B6313. Barker had a personalized means of lining up targets when shooting his Vickers machine gun. He attached a model of a red-painted devil-like creature with horns to his right-hand Vickers gun where the ring-and-bead foresight would usually have been, using the horns as a guide (see Figure 7). Such a primitive gunsight was in keeping with his instinctive shooting technique.[58] Three other pilots are known to have done this.[59] The model was originally used as a car radiator ornament or mascot.[60]

The red devil is making the gesture of thumbing his nose. Such a gesture was well-known in Britain, France, Belgium, and Italy at the time.[61] The gesture of putting the thumb to the nose dates back to circa 1903 and was used as a gesture of mockery.[62] The German flying ace Manfred von Richthofen, the Red Baron, flew a red aeroplane known as the Red Devil so the model could, perhaps, be intended to ridicule him, threatening that Barker was alert and looking for the enemy.[63]

Figure 7. *The red devil mascot. This red devil belonged to pilot Frank Bowles.* (© and courtesy of Cross & Cockade International)

Spatial Disorientation: Confusing the Senses

It was common for pilots, particularly new ones, to lose all sense of direction whilst flying in cloud and to experience great difficulty in finding their way back to their aerodrome. Pilots were advised to learn and recognize the shape of all the forests when looked at from the air as a means of orientating themselves and even to sketch maps annotated with such details for future reference.

Lieutenant Colonel Strange recollects that Australian pilots had a 'sixth sense' in that they were natural pathfinders:

> they did not need to look at a bush twice to know where it was the next time they saw it. Having flown once over a tract of country on a clear day, they would think you deserved all you got if you failed to know your whereabouts the next time you came that way just because it was a bit foggy, and I suppose they were right.[64]

A pilot flies by his visual horizon, maintaining his machine on an even keel by reference to it; an obscured horizon was not good. A pilot had an air-speed indicator and a lateral bubble (which was supposed to tell him if he was on an even keel), and 'the rest was the luck of the game and his native nouse', for: 'In a cloud there is no horizon, nothing above, below, in front, behind, but thick white mist, and many a man has fallen out of the clouds in a spin through losing his head and, without knowing it, standing his machine on its ear.'[65]

Spatial disorientation occurs when a pilot loses visual reference to the natural horizon by, for example, flying into cloud or when flying in restricted visibility and the pilot is unsure of his precise attitude in space, or where is 'up' and 'down'. His sensory image of being in the air is, accordingly, false. It has been established that feelings of tilting and turning are dangerously unreliable indicators of reality because 'at small angles of bank the plane's change of direction and position went unnoticed much of the time'.[66] Getting lost could give rise to feelings of panic, rendering the pilot unable to perform the correct manoeuvres and responses. The compasses of the day were unreliable because the vibration of the aircraft affected them. On performing a couple of turns, a pilot could easily lose his sense of direction and become disoriented for flying just one sharp turn could cause the compass to spin uncontrollably, causing much confusion for the pilot. To get round this, Cecil Lewis advised focusing on a landmark in the distance in order to allow the compass time to calm down. Once the compass had settled it was advisable to quickly look for a recognizable landmark such as a river or town and then try to pinpoint them on a map. Of course, this was easier to do:

high up than low down but whatever the height, the pilot had to have a sense of scale. Ten miles on the map looked very different in reality at a thousand or ten thousand feet, so you had to take your height into consideration when locating your position . . . it needed experience.[67]

Disorientation could be so severe that sometimes the pilots did not know whether they were flying upside down. Lieutenant Colonel Strange recollects returning from a dawn reconnaissance over enemy lines when a black snowstorm, 20,000ft high, swept in. He was quickly surrounded by pitch blackness 'in which the bumps were terrific' and it was difficult to control the aeroplane.[68] If a pilot becomes disoriented, for example, through poor visibility he uses the sound of the wind on the aeroplane and the feel of the wind on his face to orchestrate his responses as hearing and feeling have substituted for sight. Strange used the elements to his advantage:

> . . . when the wires screamed throttled back, and when I encountered momentary lull I pushed the stick forward.[69] Sometimes I felt as though I was sitting on air, while all the weight of my body was thrown on to my belt;[70] then I could do nothing, but try to think out how best to roll the machine the right way up. When I side-slipped, the fact was indicated to me by the howling draught on the side of my face.[71]

As Strange's aircraft lost height, he continued to be disorientated, and could have been flying upside down for all he knew. He relates:

> Suddenly it got quite light, and I saw snowflakes all around me. Then a church spire, upside down, hove into sight just over my top left-hand wing-tip. My instinct told me to put it the right side up, and somehow I managed to do it. The church spire flicked out of sight and then appeared on my right in a more reasonable attitude.[72]

Strange successfully learned how to interact with the aeroplane in adverse conditions that restricted his vision and to trust his bodily instincts and his understanding of the elements to instigate the correct judgments enabling a safe landing.

Reflections on Flying the Conflict Body

In Chapters 3 and 4 I have presented an alternative view of First World War aviation by describing and analysing the sensorial engagement of aviators with the aircraft they flew. By employing haptic analysis in conjunction with other senses to understand experience, a 'pilot culture', and how technology changes the sensorium, it was possible to conceptualize a First World War aviator's quotidian experiences and sensations. The foci of this conceptualization were the cultural transformations of the human body; the reconfiguration of the pilot's senses; aviators' cultural perceptions of time, space, speed, and distance; and the experience of new corporeal feelings as aviators adapted to the physical and environmental constraints afforded by flying an open-cockpit aeroplane. For a pilot, the senses of touch provide a warning system as regards his well-being, a means of communication and of verification. In terms of communicating with personnel on the ground, eventually observers were trained in Morse code, thus endowing their hands with the ability to 'speak', such re-configured 'speech' becoming tactile and silent as it grasped this new technology.

Aviators' senses were re-configured and culturally constructed as they learned to engage with a new way of moving and the human body became the 'pilot body'. The sentient pilot 'body has a history and is as much a cultural phenomenon as it is a biological entity'.[73] The First World War pilot body became 'at once tool, agent, and object'.[74]

First World War aviators saw the boundaries between man and machine seemingly dematerialize as the sentient pilot body was culturally transformed. Aeroplanes may be regarded as 'material prostheses to the human body' for they change the way the body experiences movement.[75] The technology of the aeroplane, in creating a re-modelling of the human body into the pilot body, 'eliminat[ed] the limitations of sentience . . . magnifying its powers, [to] make sentience itself an artefact'.[76]

As well as learning to fly and becoming skilful at doing so, aviators had to get to grips with the new technology of both aerial photography and wireless transmitting. Such new technology 'extends the reach of the body and can give us a sense of experiencing a world apart from the body'.[77] The use of wireless technology had an interesting effect on the senses for it provides an example of Gell's 'distributed person' as explained above. For example, as the pilot instructed the artillery batteries on the ground to more accurately direct their guns at the enemy, he was instrumental in causing men to be killed in areas nowhere near his own physical body – he had become the eyes of the army, thereby extending the scale and nature of the conflict landscape.

Technology and biology seemingly merged as the technology of aeroplanes enabled the pilot body to overcome its natural limitations. A First World War pilot learned the limits and tolerances of his body, particularly with regards to how high he could fly without, for example, the aid of an oxygen mask and the debilitating effects of the symptoms of what is now called hypoxia. The felt tolerances of an aeroplane in terms of handling capabilities were culturally important to aviators of the RFC but were not immediately apparent – they came with experience and were bodily ways of knowing in terms of representing a 'culturally constructed sensorium'.[78]

Chapter 5

Mascots, Emotions, and Flying

Flying in bad weather on the way to Metz on a bombing raid, Captain F. Williams remembered:

> I caught sight of our second raid away on my right; as I looked out, surveying the scene, I suddenly became aware of the thunder of the exhaust in my ear, the pressure of the slip-stress and the tiny fluttering Union Jack, which I carried as a mascot; all fear was lost, for one glorious moment, in a feeling of wild exultation.[1]

The idea of haptics incorporates the sense of touch in its metaphorical form, that is touching experiences that encompass emotions.[2] First World War aviators were in touch with their world through their emotions, particularly the emotions of fear and anxiety, as they turned to superstition to attract good luck and protection as a coping strategy to address such feelings in order to survive. Certainly, this view of touch becomes a useful theoretical tool when applied to the more holistic, self-reflexive, and emotional archaeologies. Pilots relied on lucky mascots to help make sense of the world. The aviator mind and body faced danger on a daily basis – not just from the enemy but from their flimsy aeroplanes that could break up in the sky with inevitable results.

Fighter pilot Arthur Gould Lee recalled that 'most of us who flew in France were scared a little, and sometimes a lot, almost every time we went into action'. Aircrew experienced emotions of fear and anxiety, for example, the fear of being hit by a bullet at any time. Indeed, Gould Lee wrote: 'No one ever talked about our secret dreads. Only obliquely, in gruesome jokes and ante-room ditties, was the spectre of fear admitted, and then but to be mockingly dismissed.'[3]

It is estimated that at least three-quarters of First World War airmen carried some kind of lucky mascot.[4] This would indicate that they were superstitious, at least to a degree. Indeed, many aviators carried more than one mascot – however, John McGavock Grider recorded that he was not superstitious although, somewhat ironically, this was the last entry in his diary before he died in aerial combat.[5] The *Oxford English Dictionary* defines superstition as 'the irrational belief in supernatural events; a belief that supernatural influences can bring good or bad luck'.[6] Physician and psychiatrist Sir Robert Armstrong-Jones recognized superstition as the 'encroachment of faith on the rights of reason and knowledge'. In 1929 it was understood that:

> Ordinarily, we reject supernatural stories because they do not fit in with the conclusions we ourselves have experienced, or the theories we have formed, yet fear, terror, or other emotions may compel us to believe in what we cannot prove or disprove to the satisfaction of our senses. Most of us are unconscious of the narrow range of our own experience and so involuntarily come to believe in superstition. Psychologically, this question is based on the instinct of fear.[7]

The First World War was unique in human history at that time because it introduced dangers and threats to human life in terms of industrialized killing and wounding (and at heights above the earth) that had never been known before. Arguably the importance and frequency of mascot usage was a predictable psychological response to these threats and therefore an integral part of investigating conflict aviators' lives and experiences.

Defining a Mascot

Undeniably humans have always been aware of the forces of good and evil and, in this awareness, derives our curiosity or faith in mascots and it is such belief that affords mascots influence or power. Originally all mascots had a religious significance; they were not worn for their own powers but in the hope that they might attract the spiritual influences that would prove beneficial to their wearers, or at least would repel or combat evil.

The *Oxford English Dictionary* defines the word mascot as being 'a person, animal, or object that is supposed to bring good luck'.[8] This may include lucky items such as amulets, talismans, and charms.[9] Such objects could be construed 'as an imagined preservative against sickness or other evils'.[10] There is no essential difference between an amulet, talisman, or charm and there is often some overlap in the meaning of the three words as they are invariably used indiscriminately.[11] But to be a little more precise, an amulet is a device that is worn for protection by magical means whereas a charm is an object that is perceived to bring good luck, health, and happiness, although it might also protect from bad luck but protection is not its primary function. A talisman, on the other hand, is something thought to hold a magic property which can both protect and radiate power.

Many RFC squadrons had a living squadron animal/human mascot as an emblem of that unit. Individual aviators also kept pets. Unless such mascots were deemed by the owner or owners as 'luck bringing', they are not lucky mascots and do not fit into the categories of lucky mascots I suggest later in this chapter.[12] For that reason, such mascots have not been included in this book, though they are an important area of study.[13]

Lucky Mascots at the Beginning of the Twentieth Century

At the beginning of the twentieth century there was a revival in the belief in luck and protective amulets as well as lucky pocket pieces, particularly 'amongst bridge-players, actors, sportsmen, motorists, gamblers, burglars, and others engaged in risky occupations'.[14] Charms in the form of horseshoes, four-leaved clovers and pigs, for example, were fashionable representing a 'half-belief' that they would bring good luck or reflect ill-luck.[15] The literature from this time informs that the word 'mascot' seemed to be more popular than the word 'amulet' or even 'talisman'.[16] It is clear that such devotion to belief in the so-called protective 'powers' of mascots carried on into the First World War as aviators and their families hoped that such things could hold magical powers that attracted luck, promised protection, or ensured safety to men serving on the Western Front.

Writing in 1907, author George Bratley wrote that, in the Roman Catholic Church, a holy vest was a gift often made by the Pope to protect the wearer from violence and that the vests gave the wearer courage in the hour of danger, and no weapon had power to harm him.[17] He fuelled the pre-war imaginations of his reading public which contributed to the popularity of lucky charms and mascots with soldiers and aviators during the First World War. Elizabeth Villiers also adds texture by explaining the meanings behind mascots in terms of lucky numbers, objects believed to be traditionally lucky such as heather, cats, the saying 'thumbs up', and the teddy bear.[18] She writes that people really did believe in mascots, although they might attempt to hide such belief, acknowledging that 'the airman carries his luck bringer in his "buss" when he attempts his greatest flights'.[19]

Social history provides insights into the wider world of superstition and its related material culture which provide a detailed context for the beliefs and activities of pilots and soldiers. Ernest Sackville (E.S.) Turner reveals how the war stimulated a trade in talismans, amulets, and sacred emblems. He relates how one individual sent 147 parcels to prisoners of war, including a Sacred Heart badge in each parcel, in the belief that the badge would ensure its safe arrival.[20] The fact that all parcels arrived safely fuelled such beliefs. Faced with subsequent huge orders for these badges from soldiers' relatives, Jesuit priests warned that it was not a talisman to ward off bullets. Nevertheless, soldiers publicly claimed that if one wore the badge and shouted 'O Sacred Heart of Jesus, have mercy on us!', bullets miraculously missed them.[21] Turner also addresses the public's rush to spiritualism but it was not just the general public that were interested. RFC pilot Geoffrey Wall, in *Letters of an Airman*, describes attending a seance in London. Although he confessed that he did not believe in spiritualism, after the seance he related how he 'felt horribly relieved – a sort of mild, morning-after-the-night before feeling, and [his] pulse seemed to be throbbing like a pile-driver'.[22]

It is perhaps the folklorist Edward Lovett who provides some of the most detailed and knowledgeable insights into amulets and lucky charms during the early twentieth century.[23] His seminal 1925 booklet *Magic in Modern London* gives examples used by First World War soldiers to ensure survival. One such example involves a conversation he had with a friend whose reply to Lovett's questioning was '[m]y dear Lovett, I can assure you there is no time out there to think of such rubbish. You have been had if you have been told such rot'. Lovett responded that 'he knew of many officers who were college men and who were carrying mascots in the war'. The friend was unconvinced, but, as he bade Lovett farewell, he removed a small box from his pocket that contained a small gold oriental figure – it was his mascot.[24] Lovett's view was that 'the more superstitious people are, the less they are inclined to talk about it'.[25] Sometimes, lucky mascots were secretly incorporated into a soldier's or airman's belongings by others. Lovett reports how a worried mother sewed a Carnelian pendant into the lining of her non-superstitious son's tunic. Her son returned from the war.[26]

Information about charms and how to use them was widely available. In 1907, Bratley advised that a charm should be used intelligently and, if seeking luck, the wearer must not just rely on the charm itself but must play his part in order to bring about the desired results.[27] For example, a pilot should practise flying his aeroplane and changing the drum on his machine gun, as John McGavock Grider recorded, 'we've practiced changing until we can do it in our sleep'.[28] Bratley even proffered advice on how to use a charm, writing, '[h]old it between the finger and thumb and gaze at it steadily or if in the dark simply hold it. Concentrate your thoughts on your highest ideal and contemplate faithfully the conditions which you desire'. Bratley suggested that such quiet meditation should be performed daily in order to attract courage, faith, and strength.[29]

The existence of mascots is driven by the human instinct to survive at all costs as the aviator confronted his mortality on a daily basis. Aircrew were aware of the odds of them dying, and trainee pilot Frederick Ortweiler wondered 'how long it will take for [him] to get the wind up', recording in his diary, 14 March 1917, '[c]heery news today in Parliament; 20% are killed in 6 weeks. We're all doomed'.[30]

Arthur Gould Lee was a pallbearer at many funerals when he was learning to fly at Filton, near Bristol. Casualties were buried in a coffin and there was a padre in attendance at the funeral during which the last post was regularly sounded as a mark of respect for the dead.[31] Its sound resonated throughout surrounding areas for all to hear and to know what was happening. Such funereal frequency caused Gould Lee to think that he had grown hardened to the death of his peers; that is until he acted as pallbearer at the funeral of a young aviator at La Gorgue cemetery on the Western Front at which no padre was in attendance, and no last post sounded, which he describes as being a 'depressing business' for his friend was not in a coffin but 'sewn up in canvas, placed on a wide plank, and covered with the Union Jack. We could feel the corpse, cold, rigid, when we took him to the graveside from the trailer. It gave me quite a turn.'[32] Gould clearly remembers his friend's funeral and such emotions are integral aspects of human cognition as aviators sensed that they could be the next to die.

Aviators and their Lucky Mascots

Not many First World War aviation-related charms and lucky mascots have found their way into museum exhibits and those that have seem to have become alienated from their human stories. The National Museum of Wales, for example, holds forty First World War lucky mascots in its archives that were donated by Lovett, in 1918.[33] Only one of these mascots is connected to aeroplanes and aviators and the typed label that accompanies it offers little information other than it was crafted from pieces of German ordnance shell and worn by flying men in France in 1917–18.

On tracking down examples of lucky mascots in museums, in photographs, on the Internet, as mentioned in books and newspaper articles, it became apparent that there were many different types of aviator-related mascots. The categorization of mascot types here is an attempt to bring order, meaning, and significance to these items and to help us understand them more than 100 years after they were made and carried (see Table 1). However, be warned, the whole process of object classification is slippery and some objects defy a one size fits all approach. Certain objects can be in several categories at the same time – it is not just one object one category.

My classification of aviators' lucky mascots was influenced by 'social history' and 'cultural history'. Turner reveals how war stimulated trade in talismans, an indication that a category entitled 'commercially made, sold as lucky charm' was required (Category A).[34] The French cultural historian Annette Becker provides insight into religion and lucky mascots which led to Category B entitled 'charm with religious significance'.[35] Additionally, it was evident from the aviators' texts that it was common to keep a piece of something connected to a crash they had survived, hence Category C entitled 'lucky pocket piece, often with survival story'. Paul Fussell in his magisterial *The Great War and Modern Memory* notes that luck depended not on what mascot a person carried but on what action a person did or did not do and it became clear that a Category D entitled 'lucky sayings, omens, and rituals' was justified.³⁶ Jude Hill notes that some of the First World War mascots in the Lovett Collection, held by the Wellcome Historical Medical Museum in London, consisted of particular forms that related to certain established superstitions.³⁷ Brooches, for example, formed in the shape of a black cat – in folklore the black cat is deemed to be lucky – and this led to Category E entitled 'objects traditionally associated with good luck in folklore'.³⁸ Finally, Chambers acknowledges the variety in the range of lucky mascots and beliefs, and it was apparent that aviators often afforded their own meanings to objects that held special significance to them, and so Category F 'personal objects infused with special/intimate meaning, personal to the aviator' was an important addition to the list.³⁹

Table 1: Aviators' Lucky Mascots, Omens, Sayings, and Rituals: Categories of Superstition

Category	Examples	Comments	Percentage of Research Sample
A. Commercially made, sold as a lucky charm	Small metal charm of aeroplane; Fum's Up! charm; Nénette and Rintintin charms; charm in the guise of something traditionally associated with good luck, e.g. cat, boomerang, Fum's Up! doll.	Popular mass-produced trinket. Given as a gift to wish recipient 'Good Luck'.	14%
B. Charms with religious significance	St Christopher; prayer chain; crucifix inside leather case worn over heart; thumb-size copy of 91st Psalm or Lord's Prayer.	(i) either given to aviator; or (ii) chosen by aviator.	7%
C. Lucky pocket pieces, often with survival story	A piece of shrapnel from a crash which the pilot survived; a bullet taken from a wound which the aviator survived; a small piece of trench art made from pieces of a survived crash; something 'souvenired' from an enemy aeroplane that the pilot caused to crash, e.g. a silk hat or helmet from a German aviator (war trophy).	An aviator exercised his own agency, for example, in re-labelling a bullet that had hit him but not killed him as a lucky pocket piece to signify his survival.	14%

Category	Examples	Comments	Percentage of Research Sample
D. Lucky sayings, omens, and rituals	Lucky sayings, e.g. 'touch wood'; lucky way of saying 'au revoir', particularly by Americans – 'see you in hell'. Interpreting omens, e.g. behaviour of cigarette smoke; numbers. Bodily ritual, e.g. turn clockwise three times before climbing into aeroplane.	Such superstitions derived: (i) from folklore; or (ii) the aviator invented it. Often the belief in something particular was of a personal nature. Such superstitions may have an anthropological interpretation.	11%
E. Objects traditionally associated with good luck in folklore	Lucky heather, particularly white; four-leaf clover; image of cat painted on aeroplane for good luck; toy in the guise of something traditionally associated with good luck, e.g. cat.	(i) often given as a gift to wish good luck from mother, sister, sweetheart; or (ii) pilot decided which folklore to adopt.	15%
F. Personal object infused with special/intimate meaning, personal to the aviator	Small toy from a friend, e.g. teddy bear; photo of someone special; glass dog from Christmas cracker; miniature crocheted woollen baby's bootees; pocket edition of 'The Happy Warrior'; a favourite item of clothing that the pilot would never dream of flying without.	Such items were either: (i) personal to the aviator in that he already owned it and he decided it would bring him good luck; or (ii) had special personal meaning, perhaps memories, given as a gift to the pilot to bring luck.	39%

Chapter 6

The Surreal World of Flying

Imagine a surreal world of men ruled by superstition. In this world were good omens and bad omens as men participated in rituals as a means of encouraging and attracting good fortune. Their families lived elsewhere but they sent their men lucky mascots. The men painted black cats on aeroplanes with huge wingspans they flew at night. Their world was frightening and unpredictable and they had a precise set of unwritten instructions for survival. They believed that misery would befall them if they did not follow the rules and forgot to take their protective mascots with them. The following description and analysis systematically unravels this world as it explores how superstition became tangible reality in the form of rituals, omens, and objects.

Here, the different types of mascots carried by First World War airmen are explored to reveal how an object can present wider associations and entanglements with material things whilst structuring the wider social networks of relationships beyond the RFC.

Commercially Made, Sold as a Lucky Charm

Industrial warfare stimulated a consumer industry as commercially made charms were made to be given to aviators as a gift to wish 'good luck' as manufacturers sought to make a profit from the commercialization of superstition by war. Commercial advertisers in journals and periodicals relied on the public's 'belief in "luck" and in obtaining it by things said or done or worn'.[1] The following are examples of commercially made charms.

Kewpie Dolls and Fum's Up! Charms
The poet and artist Rose O'Neill drew cartoon-type pictures of Cupid-like figures called Kewpie dolls which first appeared in magazine illustrations in 1909.[2] These were later patented in 1913 by the manufacturing company J.D. Kestner based in Waltershausen, Germany. The name Kewpie derives from their resemblance to the naked babies known as cupids, after Cupid the Roman god of love. Over the next

few years, the Kewpies grew in popularity; books and accessories were introduced including, soap dishes and salt and pepper shakers. Though initially manufactured in Germany, the Kewpies were later made in Belgium and France following the outbreak of the First World War. Their popularity continued to increase, the Kewpie doll being one of the earliest examples of mass manufacturing. Royal Flying Corps pilot Geoffrey Wall, in a letter to his sister, was of the opinion that the name 'Kewpie' sounded like a brand of sardines![3]

Raphael Tuck & Sons was one of the earliest postcard publishers, introducing the Oilette series of paintings on postcards – where the surface was designed to appear as a miniature painting – in 1903. The company had been established by Jewish Prussian husband and wife immigrants, Raphael and Ernestine Tuck. Raphael Tuck died in 1900 but the business was carried on by his sons who made postcards a very popular means of communication.[4] Raphael Tuck & Sons was adroit in recognizing and responding to the country's mood and fashions and, in response to people's evident interest in luck and the popularity of the Kewpie dolls, and because the First World War was now raging and feelings of patriotism running high, it published the Fum's Up! postcard so that people could send each other good luck. Unfortunately, on 29 December 1940, its headquarters were bombed and 74 years' worth of archives in the form of over 40,000 original pictures and photographs were destroyed but an example of a Fum's Up! postcard is reproduced here (Figure 8, Plate 2).

We use our body to make meaningful gestures of communication and our body biologically emits signs and signals as to its well-being. The phrase 'thumbs up' was a popular saying at the turn of the twentieth century, an upturned thumb signifying encouragement to do one's best in order for events to turn out successfully.[5] The name 'Fum's Up!' is a take on the gesticulatory action of 'thumbs up', attributing the gesture to the action of a Roman emperor as to whether a gladiator lives or dies, the position of the thumb, either up or down, being a matter of life or death respectively – although historians disagree with this for thumbs up may have meant an unpleasant insult and it was thumbs down that signified a pleasant form of approval.[6] But this is what the publisher of the postcards believed at the time. It is therefore a legacy of ancient materiality, linking actions from the ancient world with objects of the First World War and thereby shaping human experience.

A popular superstition in Britain today, that can be traced to the early nineteenth century, concerns touching wood and/or saying 'touch wood' after boasting or tempting fate, in order to avert ill-luck.[7] Due to the popularity of these postcards, three-dimensional style metal figures were commercially mass-produced, some with wooden heads, for touching, to bring good luck (saying 'touch wood' is considered further in Chapter 7). The purchaser would send such figurines to their loved ones serving on the Western Front and many of them found their way into the pockets of RFC aviators. Some of the examples of Fum's Up! figures had

Figure 8. *Verso of the postcard describing FUMS UP! From the Fum's Up! set, Oilette Series Postcard No. 8792A.* (Author's collection)

lucky birthstone eyes that sparkled 'as if always on the alert to see and avert danger', just as an aviator would be when flying (see Plate 3).[8]

Pilot Vernon Castle wrote in a letter to his wife: 'Your letter . . . received this morning. Thank you ever so much . . . The Kewpie soldier . . . I haven't received yet'.[9] The 'Kewpie soldier' that Castle refers to was probably a Fum's Up! charm.

The charms were made by American jewellery company J.M. Fisher Company of Attelboro, Bristol County, Massachusetts. The packaging of the Fum's Up! charm is of particular significance as the charm is placed on cardboard printed with the Union Jack and a 'John Bull' character, both representing patriotic times and themes.[10] A lucky four-leaf clover was imprinted on the forehead of the charm and the arms were jointed so that they could be raised to touch the wooden head, a design feature to emulate the popular custom of touching wood 'when hopes are expressed, so as not to tempt the fates and bring disappointment'.[11] This custom is thought to derive from the ancient Catholic veneration of the True Cross.[12]

The printed message that accompanied the Fum's Up! charm informs that it is made to bring luck and that it is actually a combination of two charms, 'touch wood' and Fum's Up!:

> My head is made
> Of wood most rare,
> My thumbs turn up
> To touch me there.
> To speed my feet
> They've Cupid's wings,
> They'll help true love
> 'Mongst other things.
> Proverbial is
> My power to bring
> Good luck to you
> In everything.
> I'll bring good luck
> To all away—
> Just send me to
> A friend to-day.

Such charms were widely available, and advertisements regularly appeared in popular newspapers and magazines (see Figure 9).

It was not just members of the RFC who were superstitious – Air Mechanic Henry James Marston, of No. 3 Squadron, Australian Flying Corps, was particularly superstitious and wore a bracelet comprising an identity tag with three commercially made lucky charms attached – a boomerang, a Fum's Up! charm, and a black cat.[13] The identity tag personalizes the three charms and bears Marston's name as well as his mother's name and address on the back. Perhaps his mother gave it to him to ensure his safe return to her. The boomerang, firmly established in popular perception as an Australian icon, is in the shape of a 'returning' boomerang and is engraved with the words 'I go to Return' clearly stating his hope to survive the war and return home to Australia. Every time Marston moved his wrist, he would have been aware of the charms, feeling the cold metal on his skin and, perhaps, was reminded of his faraway home, endowing geographic space and distance with meaning. The charms, worn round Marston's wrist, are imbued with his wartime experiences.

Fate appears to have been on Marston's side for he narrowly escaped being hit by an aeroplane that crash-landed and exploded at the squadron's aerodrome close to where he was standing. He survived the war and returned to Australia in June

Figure 9. *An advertisement displaying three types of good-luck charms and mascots.* (© Illustrated London News Ltd/Mary Evans)

1919. The bracelet of charms is now exhibited at the Australian War Memorial, although now it is just an item in a glass display case for it has lost its significance and meaning as a lucky charm and has become a museum exhibit instead, another event in its 'social' life.[14]

Nénette and Rintintin
Illustrator Francisque Poulbot created drawings of two Paris street children, a girl and a boy, naming them Nénette and Rintintin. The drawings were then used to design two dolls which the manufacturers intended to replace the dolls sold in French shops that were made in Germany – signifying an act of patriotism. The dolls were especially popular before the outbreak of war but production initially slowed at the start of hostilities. However, the characters were revived during the war in a book entitled *Encores des Gosses et des Bonhommes: cent dessins et l'histoire de Nénette et Rintintin* (*More Kids and Men. One Hundred Drawings and the Story of Nénette and Rintintin*) (see Figure 10).[15]

Figure 10. *A sketch by Francisque Poulbot detailing a street child playing with Nénette and Rintintin charms.* (Author's collection)

Nénette and Rintintin were associated with luck:

> Everyone loves and adores us. You can find us amongst the finest amulets, the hand of Fatima, four-leaved clover, golden pigs, scarab beetles, the number 13, and white elephants . . . We are the popular good-luck-charm that protects Parisiennes from the Gotha bombs and the big canon's shells! . . . we triumph over bad luck . . . Place us round your neck, on your watch chain, on your bracelet, in your pocket, on your car's windshield. With us you will never become ill, never get killed . . . Touch wood! [author's translation][16]

They were charms made from scraps of yarn that were joined together and apparently had to remain attached to retain their protective powers. Nénette and Rintintin were characterized as an adult couple, sometimes with a baby, who survived the Gotha attacks and bombardments. Very quickly, small wool versions of the dolls were created, purchased, and given to soldiers and airmen on the Western Front as good luck charms (see Plate 4). The Nénette and Rintintin charms were pinned upon clothes or attached to hats, or even sent home to the United Kingdom as souvenirs.

The RAF Museum London archives hold twenty letters from Eric Randall Lloyd Sproule to his mother covering the entire period of his service and captivity, from 1 January 1917 to 4 December 1918, including a letter and small fabric charm of the characters Nénette and Rintintin. Eric wrote in a letter:

> My dearest Mother
> . . . I enclose for you what is all the rage in France at the moment, everyone has got these, they are called 'Nénette' and 'Rintintin' and they originated in Paris as a charm against the 'Gothas' and the bombardment. Keep them as a souvenir. Love to all . . .
>
> Ever your loving son,
> Eric xxxx[17]

Eric did not use the charm for himself, for it was only considered lucky if given as a gift. Eric chose to send it to his mother as a souvenir as he witnessed the charms fuelling the French citizens' superstition. Eric is giving an intimate part of himself to his mother, an embodiment of his personal off-duty time during which he purchased the charm. The letter would have been written during a quiet time as he reflected on his day and wrote to his mother. No doubt, from time to time, Eric's mother carefully removed his letters from the envelopes, re-read them, and touched the Nénette and Rintintin charm as she thought of her son, hoping he was safe and well. However, according to John McGavock Grider, such charms may not have been that lucky, writing in his diary: 'I saw Springs the other day in Boulogne. He said his girl at home sent him a pair of . . . Ninette and Rintintin luck charms. Since then he's lost five men, been shot down twice himself.'[18] Such is superstition.

Personal Objects Infused with Special/Intimate Meaning Personal to the Aviator

Mascots were often infused with special meaning in that they were given as a gift from, perhaps, a wife, girlfriend, friend, or close family member, and so invoked intimate personal relationships. Such mascots were often kept safe after the war, acting as a reminder of the noise of the bullets, the visual scar of being hit by a bullet, the smell of the fuel or the sudden silence from the engine cutting out. Memory is after all 'the horizon of sensory experience'.[19]

The lucky mascot 'Sunny Jim' (see Plate 6) was always carried by RFC pilot Gerard Gwyn Crutchley (see Figure 11). This act indicated a sensory relationship with the mascot, which seemingly provided a feeling of comfort, enabling Gerard to reflect on the memorable day it was presented to him by the actress and comedienne Beatrice Lillie in 1917.[20] She wrote 'Good Luck' and signed her name. He described the meeting in a letter to a friend:

> I met a little Peach in town about 10 days ago and have had two glorious days with her already. She is on the stage and unfortunately has just started touring. This week she is in Folkestone. She is coming to London again soon though. Will tell you all about it when I see you.[21]

Made of a golden yellow fabric, Sunny Jim is a fictitious character. His head looks like a sun, hence the name. The significance of the sun talisman is culturally a longstanding one – as the symbol of life, and thus, as a mascot, it ensures health and success and power, particularly to those born under the birth sign Leo.[22] Coincidentally, Crutchley was born on 8 August 1893 under Leo, such astrological interpretation being an example of divination in the modern Western world.

Gerard Crutchley's sensory relationship with the mascot is linked to his memory of the day the actress gave it to him. On 10 July 1917, his head was struck by his aeroplane propeller causing fractures to his skull. His family were informed that he may not recover, but remaining in hospital for nearly one month, he survived his accident and returned to train pilots.

German airmen also held beliefs in the protective power of things. Indeed, German fighter pilot Manfred von Richthofen's family donated a blue-hued glass dog to the RAF Museum, London. Richthofen was fond of dogs and it is alleged that he believed that, as long as the glass dog remained in his possession, he would escape injury.

Figure 11. *RFC pilot Gerard Gwyn Crutchley.* (© Gerry Crutchley)

But, whilst convalescing from an injury, he gave the glass dog to his nurse. He was subsequently shot in the chest during a dogfight and died shortly after giving away the mascot.[23] The glass dog is reminiscent of a Dachshund, a dog used to scent, chase, and flush out burrow-dwelling animals; perhaps Richthofen thought it would help him flush out Allied pilots in the skies.

The dog is made from Czech glass and such small figures were traditionally placed in Christmas crackers. The glass dog could therefore have been a reminder of a happy family Christmas on Richthofen's father's estate in Silesia, Prussia, thus highlighting an association to happy festive family memories from home textured with the smells of Christmas. However, other sources suggest that Richthofen did not believe in lucky charms, and, when someone suggested a charm, he was quick to respond that his Spandau machine guns were his lucky mascot.[24] Folklorist Edward Lovett's view was that the more superstitious people are, the less inclined they are to talk or admit to being superstitious.[25]

Lucky Pocket Pieces, Often with Survival Story

Chance often determined what the lucky pocket piece would be, for example, an ornament that happened to be worn on a particularly successful hunting expedition may in consequence come to be looked upon as an object assuring corresponding good fortune on similar occasions in the future, or another may analogously become a charm promising success in warfare.[26] Gordon Taylor carried the piece of Archie shell which had been extracted from the wing of his aeroplane in the pocket of his flying coat. The jagged shrapnel was roughly an inch square in size and Taylor's colleague had found it wedged in his damaged aeroplane. Taylor wrote, '[t]he war was suddenly very real indeed. I weighed the piece of steel in my hand and dropped it into the pocket of my flying coat, where it stayed'.[27] Taylor hoped that his good fortune in surviving on this occasion would repeat itself on a similar encounter in the future. It was believed that for objects to bring good luck, the man who carried it must have survived a campaign. Clearly it was chance that determined what the lucky pocket piece would be, but, whatever it was, it was viewed as an object that assured success and survival in conflict.

John McGavock Grider wrote that he retained a piece of his first crash for luck even though he maintained that he was not superstitious.[28] The written words of the pilot are extremely important because they apportion meaning and significance to the piece of Archie. If that particular piece of metal had been found during an archaeological excavation, its significance as a lucky pocket piece would not have been apparent due to the abundance of such objects.

Lieutenant B.C. Hucks Small retained a splinter of the propeller which burst on his machine and nearly cost him his life, when he was flying for his aviator's certificate at the beginning of his career.[29] He did so in the belief and hope that it would keep him safe during the war. He exercised his own 'agency' in re-labelling the splinter of propeller as a lucky pocket piece which signifies his feat of surviving that particular flight.[30]

It was common for aviators to carry more than one lucky pocket piece. Lieutenant Robert Loraine was an actor as well as a pilot before joining the RFC. He carried an old pair of leather gloves with him when he flew. The gloves had a survival story attached to them for it is reported that he wore these gloves during his attempt to fly the Irish Channel before the war, and had the misfortune to fall into the sea. He had to swim nearly a mile to the shore.[31] The gloves accompanied him when he flew during the First World War, which he survived, although he did experience dangerous moments.

On his first reconnaissance Loraine flew through heavy rifle fire, and, upon landing, found fourteen bullet holes in his aeroplane, two of them only 12in from his head. On another occasion, he was shot whilst flying and, as a result of his injuries, he lost a lung.[32] Loraine always flew with the bullets that had been removed from his lung. He kept them in his breast pocket alongside a thumb-size copy of the 91st Psalm and a pocket edition of 'The Happy Warrior'.[33] Loraine's life and death experiences and emotions were seemingly imbued in these objects. The bullets are a reminder of what could have been – they could have killed him but instead they signify his survival of the bullets' deadly intent whilst remaining a reminder of the injury which left him with one functioning lung. If he were to catch cold, it would threaten to settle on his only lung making him seriously ill. However, even with such an injury, Loraine was deemed 'lucky' because, due to the nature of the injury, at the end of every seven weeks, five days attributed to health were added to the seven days' leave back in England.[34]

Although bodily experience is subjective, the concept of the sentient pilot body became an artefact of war, an object to be broken, and an object to be mended and recycled to return to being a human agent of conflict. The bullets were also recycled, not as souvenirs of war, but as lucky charms.

It was common during the First World War to remove war objects of interest from crash sites as souvenirs or trophies of war. Indeed, 'it is the wish of most pilots to bring Germans down in our lines, so as to get souvenirs from the machine'.[35] Lieutenant Rainey shot down a German aviator whilst flying over enemy lines. He took the German pilot's helmet and wore it as a lucky mascot.[36] McCudden made an entry in his diary that he wore a silk cap belonging to a German pilot that had been removed from his crashed German aeroplane. The silk cap was such a good fit that he had it copied in silk khaki and wore it in France for several months.[37] These are instances of airmen exercising their own agency in attributing objects of war with meaning and significance beyond their original purpose.

Pocket pieces can, as we have seen, be almost anything and may even belong to a different category of conflict-related object. Such is the case with an example of trench art (see Plate 5) made in the image of a twin-engine biplane typical of the era – its configuration representative of the Handley Page bomber used by both the RNAS and the RFC from late 1916. Recognizing this configuration is important because Handley Pages were used as night bombers against strategic German targets such as coastal and industrial areas and railways. The Handley Page was fitted with an early bomb aimer and five Lewis machine guns for defence. The sight of the Handley Page flying would have been memorable for it had a huge wingspan – 114ft – and no aeroplane as big as this had been seen before. Maurice Baring, adjutant to Hugh Trenchard, commander of the RFC, reported in a letter, dated 2 July 1918:

> The night before last we went to see the machines start and come back from the night expeditions to Hunland. It is quite uncanny to see the great monsters fly off into the sunset, and also disappear, and then you hear them humming in the darkness and circling round like great moths till they land . . . And how well they land! An electric light is turned on for a second from the control platform, and there is the machine safely on the ground![38]

This piece of trench art is made from copper combining a rectangular copper nail and soft copper strip (probably scrap) cut and fashioned to form wings and the twin tail plane which are silver soldered into position. Made from the metal wastes of war, this example of trench art incorporates 'the agents of death and destruction directly into its . . . artistic form'.[39]

There is no provenance for this item which was purchased on eBay. The reason I bought it is that I wanted to be able to touch a genuine war object, and not be forced to gaze at one through a glass display cabinet in a museum. Clearly there could be a question of authenticity but, at the very least, the raw material would have been around at the time for each squadron's aerodrome had a workshop to make official and unofficial items. But it would be impossible to know for sure where the scraps of metal came from. The maker may have bartered something in exchange for the scraps.

The Handley Page trench-art item, as well as being a lucky pocket piece, is also a personal memory object of flying at night as it represents personal experience of an event. Observer Second Lieutenant Roy Shillinglaw of No. 100 Squadron, for example, recalls flying a Handley Page over Metz in Germany on a full moonlit night at about 2,000ft. He could clearly see the deserted streets. He then flew 20 miles further north to Thionville with its large blast furnaces and electric power station. He saw a great firework display of bombs bursting and intense anti-aircraft and the whole sky was lit up by searchlights. On another full moonlit night, Shillinglaw remembers flying over a lake and thought that he and his observer had spotted a German aeroplane below so dived onto it only to find it was their own aeroplane's shadow.[40] Night flying played tricks, altering peoples' perception, making them see things that were not there.

The blank canvas on the nose of the Handley Pages was often artistically decorated. No. 207 Squadron RAF was known as the Black Cat Squadron and images of a black cat were often painted on its Handley Pages for it was believed to be a suitable good-luck symbol for a night bomber, especially as folklore deems that cats have nine lives.

Chapter 7

Touching Magic: Omens and Ritual

Lucky Sayings, Omens, and Rituals

Whilst aviators' ritual behaviour could be of an individual nature, there were superstitions and rituals that were distinctive to an entire squadron reinforcing their comradeship and identifying them. In many squadrons, for example, there was always a place associated with bad omens. No doubt such places – perhaps a building or a pilot's bed – were initially connected to the death of a pilot, the death subsequently creating the superstition. The short lifetime of Western Front pilots doubtless contributed to such situations. John McGavock Grider described the death of a comrade who was flying when his aeroplane's wings dropped off at 5,000ft, writing: 'He and Springs have been rooming together and that's the second roommate he's lost in two weeks. He doesn't want to ask anyone else to room with him but Reed Landis said he's not superstitious and moved in.'[1] Aviators used such death-related stories to fuel superstition. Superstition could be unique to a squadron as indicated by William MacLanachan (writing under the pseudonym 'McScotch') who recorded that in his No. 43 Squadron there was a superstition that any pilot who played the scratched and battered piano that stood in a corner of the mess would not survive the week if he touched the keys.[2] Such ritual behaviour contributing to a squadron's unique cultural identity.

There was a lucky way of saying 'au revoir' during 1917 and 1918, especially amongst American airmen. As the pilot clambered into the cockpit, he waved and shouted 'see you in hell!'.[3] It was almost as if acknowledging that his death was likely but that if he said it out loud, he might somehow survive. Evidently most charms, mascots, and talismans are real objects. But they can be an act, such as, in the case of a charm, saying 'white rabbits' on the first of the month to encourage good luck and to bring health and happiness.[4] Indeed, after air mechanics had checked the guns and engines 'they helped us into our cockpits and saw us settled into our seats and safety belts fastened, then they climbed down with a quiet, "Good luck sir"'.[5] Of course a simple everyday 'good luck' could be deemed as tempting fate.

Taylor remembers entertaining a captured German pilot in the Officer's Mess. The German made a speech and, upon raising his glass to make a toast said 'Hals und Beinbruch' which means 'may you break your neck and legs'. In the German Air Force it was perceived to be bad luck if you wished somebody good luck.[6] It was the same in Britain. In telling somebody to injure themselves, one is meaning that you really hoped the injuries did not happen and it was preferable to return home wounded from the war rather than dead. Saying good luck could bring bad luck so 'break a leg' was used instead so that an injury would not occur.

Touching wood is probably one of the best-known superstitions in Britain today. We touch wood and/or we say 'touch wood' at the same time whenever we have tempted fate in some way or been boastful. For many people such an action is practically involuntary and part of everyday life and speech, as indeed is 'good luck' and 'break a leg'. Clearly the act of touching wood along with its superstitious meaning is not visible in the archaeological record and it is to the words of the people who were there that we turn. Pilot Norman Macmillan writes that it was not advisable to say anything with certainty without touching wood, otherwise the opposite would happen or a run of good luck could change to bad.[7]

First World War pilots often used the phrase 'touch wood', adding resonance in the First World War because aircraft were made of wood. Indeed, Arthur Gould Lee wrote, 'I touched wood, glued my eyes to the Aldis, took aim on the Hun'.[8] Gould Lee was asked why he touched wood instead of praying before a fight. He replied in a letter:

> [W]hy should God grant me any special favour? The Hun I'm fighting may be calling on him too. It isn't as though I have any great faith in religion, but even if I had, would it divert a bullet? . . . How can I call on God to help me shoot down a man in flames?
>
> But you do need something to stiffen you. Maybe some fellows do appeal to God. Others are just superstitious, have charms or cross their fingers, or, like me, touch wood. That's different. You're asking chance not to lay the odds too much against you. It's a kind of talisman to ward off evil.[9]

On occasion, some pilots seemingly broke the ritual and forgot to touch wood. Since his first solo flight at Shoreham during which he touched wood, Duncan Grinnell-Milne kept up the ritual on future flights. However, on one flight, asked '[d]o you think we are scheduled to "go west" tomorrow?', Grinnell-Milne said:[10]

Not on my life, I maintained stoutly, would anything disastrous occur. If we went at all, and the weather made it uncertain, we would return just as we had done from a score of previous flights across the lines. My leave was due at Christmas and on that day I had every intention of dining at home. I laughed at his fears. But I must have forgotten to touch wood.[11]

The aeroplane crashed and he became a prisoner of war. He must have wondered if this was because he had not touched wood.

Belief is an individual matter and pilots regarded certain incidents or rituals as attracting good or bad omens. Airmen were anxious over the uncertainty of the time they would die and attempted to alleviate this doubt by searching for a predictable outcome. They created innovative means in an attempt to attract good fortune. Belief in propitious directions, for example, was apparent. Norman MacMillan remembers that some airmen would not drink from a bottle until the first drop had been spilled on the floor and when the bottle was passed around the other airmen, it had to be passed from left to right.[12] In other words, in the direction of the sun, to the source of life – to the right or clockwise.[13] This was deemed to be the lucky way.[14] In comparison, in the wider world, the ancient Chinese protocol of *feng shui* advises people how to decide orientations in, for instance, garden design, such directions determining a desired outcome.[15]

Such issues are of course of global distribution and trans-cultural. On observing the Maori in New Zealand, Robert Hertz's work on polarity in dexterity equates the right side of the body as being 'the side of life (and strength) while the left is the side of death (and of weakness). Fortunate and life-giving influences enter us from the right and through our right side; and, inversely, death and misery penetrate to the core of our being from the left'.[16] French sociologist Pierre Bourdieu's anthropological exploration of the lived domestic environment of an Algerian Kabyle House, introduces *habitus* concepts in terms of a series of binary oppositions that structured the occupants' lives.[17] He noted how individuals performed actions in accordance with cardinal orientation in order to achieve a particular favourable outcome. It is clear that there is a remarkable congruence between Kabyle actions designed for a positive result and those of First World War pilots who developed ways of behaving to secure a similarly favourable outcome, despite there being no objective (scientific) reason for doing so.

The practice of divination is evident in both ancient and modern civilizations and it was evidently adopted by aviators. Some pilots, for example, regarded the movement of cigarette smoke as an omen that indicated the success or failure of their next flight. If smoke was seen to move in an upwards direction, this was an indication that a pilot's next flight would go smoothly. If, however, the smoke did not appear to move in a particular direction, this caused some worry as to the success of a pilot's next flight. If smoke was witnessed to move towards the ground, this caused great worry in that it was perceived to be a signal indicating that a pilot's next flight may not be successful.[18] The action of the smoke is functioning as a code; it emits a message interpreted by the young airmen. This omen may derive from the superstition that when chimney smoke goes to the ground, bad weather will follow. Clearly, divination was associated with the pilot's sense of danger and its omission might have serious consequences.

It was within an aviator's control 'to bring this luck on himself, provided he acquires the necessary magical lore'.[19] One pilot insisted on having the number seven on all his flying gear, whilst another dreaded odd numbers on everything.[20] This despite the fact that most odd numbers have always been considered to be lucky whilst even numbers are unlucky.[21] Evidently, whilst Numerology had an ancient lineage, the rules were constructed to suit personal interpretation. Norman Macmillan, for example, reports that some airmen would not sit down with thirteen at a table and would also refuse to fly an aeroplane with a number like '3523', the units of which add up to thirteen.[22]

Whilst it was considered unlucky to fly with another man's mascot or lucky charm, some airmen refused to fly at all if they lost their own. Gordon Taylor brings to life a serious incident when his flying comrade, nicknamed Ratter, lost his lucky charm whilst swimming in the sea and refused to fly without it. Taylor recalls that Ratter was an extremely popular member of the squadron so everyone empathized with his loss and Taylor could understand his feelings very well for he too carried lucky mascots and wrote:

> We . . . searched the edge of the sea where the waves breaking on the sand left behind odds and ends washed up on the beach . . . We moved out into the shallows, sifting the sand with our fingers, digging in with our toes, trying to feel for something small and solid that could put the Ratter back in his Sopwith Pup, confident again in the magic effect of his charm. . . . we went on, not caring to stop and face the dismal truth. Then suddenly there was a shout of triumph . . . one of us found it in the sand under his feet.[23]

Aircrew participated in rituals and believed in omens and lucky sayings as a means of encouraging good luck. Such a strategic way of acting proffers a view of the cultural dynamics with which people make and remake their worlds, particularly in times of conflict.[24]

Objects Traditionally Associated with Good Luck in Folklore

White heather is traditionally associated with good luck. A sprig of white heather is quite rare to find. It is classed as a mascot considered to afford protection from danger if one happens 'to light on [white heather] while a wish was in [one's] mind, then that wish would come true'.[25] A sprig of white heather, stapled to paper signed in fountain pen 'Mickey April 1917', was sent to Major Alfred John Mitchel-Clarke by his mother and he carried it as a lucky charm.[26] Mitchel-Clarke learned to fly in a Maurice Farman biplane, receiving his aviator's certificate on 30 May 1915.[27] The message in this good luck charm is intended to preserve life. Heather is a fragile flower; it discolours, dries up and dies, just like human beings. But this heather has been preserved, albeit in a dried state, just as it was Mitchel-Clarke's mother's wish that his life be preserved. His mother's action of sending the white heather card as an 'agent' of good luck intends to change the world as she hopes it will cause her son to survive the war. Also, in accepting the gift of white heather, Mitchel-Clarke has an obligation of reciprocity in that he must survive the war – which he did.[28]

Some pilots carried toys in the image of a black cat in the hope of attracting luck. A figure of a black cat, for example, could be attached to the top of an aviator's flying helmet, altering the way he presents himself to the world – and perhaps hoping that he would lay claim to the perceived nine lives of a cat. Gordon Taylor remembers his mother giving him a fabric toy in the form of a small black cat as a mascot. He attached it to his aeroplane's instrument panel. Taylor recalls that the cat had comical whiskers and it used to look at him 'with a kind of humorous disdain which made [him] feel like a damned fool for being scared of Archie'.[29] The sight of Taylor's black cat seemingly maintained his morale.

The British fighter ace Flight Commander Captain Albert Ball VC, DSO, MC also carried a black velvet cat as a lucky mascot. At home, on leave before returning to France, Ball was presented with the cat by a young girl who called at his father's house. She made a specific request that he fasten the cat to the front of his aeroplane as a mascot. He accepted the mascot and, in a letter home, reported that it was bringing him luck.[30] Clearly the giving of gifts for luck makes specific relations with people apparent. The person who gives the mascot becomes, in anthropological terms, an 'agent' who intends for the mascot to protect the aviator, causing him to be safe.[31] Such agency had great significance in the social world of the airmen. Also, whilst Ball was an acknowledged ace, he was perhaps not so confident that he would say no to a little help from a lucky mascot. Ball did not survive the war but was thought of as one of 'the most brilliant air fighters of the war . . . His deeds were the outcome partly of pluck – certainly not of luck – but mostly of thought, insight, experiment, and constant practice'.[32]

Charms with Religious Significance

Prayer books, single prayers, and copies of the New Testament became very popular after reports that such religious works had stopped machine-gun bullets, shaping airmen's attitude to spirituality and well-being.[33] Henry Allingham carried a Bible which had been given to him by his wife, Dorothy.[34] On the inside cover, she wrote, 'May the Lord watch between thee and me while we are absent from one another. With all my fondest love and very best wishes for your welfare, Dorothy'.[35] Dorothy placed pressed flowers between the pages which evidently brought great comfort to him during the years of the war. The Bible and the dead flowers survived with him, becoming treasured heirlooms to the family after his death in 2009.

American pilot ace, Captain Eddie Rickenbacker, of the 94th Aero Squadron, wore a crucifix inside a leather case, placed over his heart.[36] Though it was hidden from general view, Rickenbacker was clearly aware of it as he flew on missions and, perhaps, would be comforted by its felt presence and by the thought that it was probably given to him by a loved one in America, a place he would hope to return to safely.

An amulet is carried for protection. St Christopher is the patron saint of travellers and the wearing of his image is a declaration of faith and belief.[37] The St Christopher seen in Plates 7 and 8 was worn by an unidentified aviator in the United States Army Air Service, perhaps around his neck or attached to his goggle straps or flying helmet. This particular amulet bears an engraved message: 'I am a Catholic, in case of an accident notify a priest'. Evidently, the aviator's religious faith was of importance to him and, in the event of being shot down, the inscription is directing that the correct religious authority should be notified. But in reality this would not happen and a religious man of any denomination may have attended, if at all, on account of there being too many deaths to deal with.

On 4 June 1916, Vernon Castle wrote to his wife, 'I've got your little prayer chained to my neck on the watch chain you gave me last Xmas. I have worn it ever since I received it, and I shall keep it on until I come back to you darling'. On 16 June 1916, Vernon wrote that the letter prayer is 'getting a little "grubby" now. I can only get a bath twice a week, but that's considered very often here in France'.[38] Here we get a small snippet of information about life on the Western Front imbuing the letter prayer with embodied experience (see Figure 12).

It was common for aviators to carry more than one lucky charm or mascot and religious amulets were mixed with non-religious ones. Castle wrote to his wife, '[y]our letter . . . received this morning and also a little gold aeroplane'.[39] The aeroplane may have looked like the one in Plate 9.

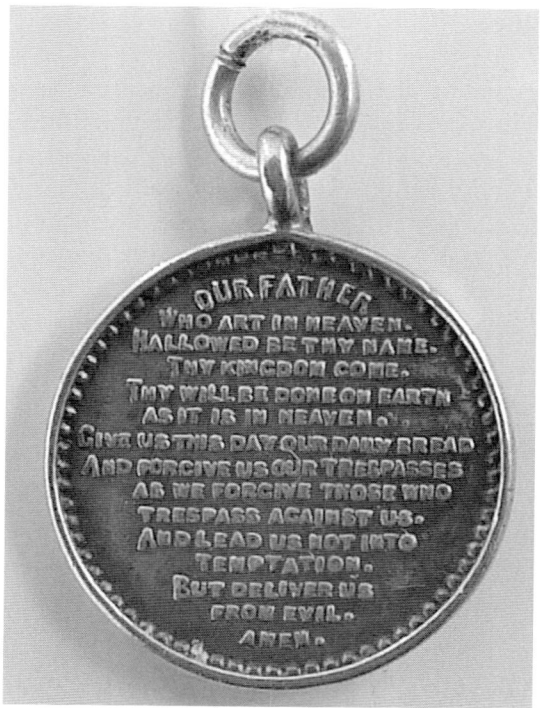

Figure 12. *An example of the Lord's Prayer on a sterling silver disk to be worn on a chain. Dimensions: diameter: 13mm.* (© Author)

The sight and sound of aeroplanes over the Western Front was commonplace. People heard the engine of the aeroplanes and they could smell the castor oil used in some of them as a lubricant.[40] It was not unusual therefore for aeroplanes to be miniaturized as charms. The aeroplane 'charm' in Plate 9 is stored in the archives of the Imperial War Museum, London. It is described as an object that has been made with the intention of being sold as a lucky charm. It is devoid of provenance, but the following offers a degree of insight. Of particular importance is the date, 1916, stamped on the charm's tail plane. This was the year of the Battle of the Somme which lasted from 1 July to 18 November 1916, some 141 days. It is regarded as one of the bloodiest battles of the First World War for 1 million men were killed and wounded on all sides. The Somme offensive commenced with gas and smoke and a bombardment of unprecedented severity that battered all the senses. Such lucky charms, particularly when date-stamped, can be associated with particular historic dates of importance and are representative of perceived sensorial experiences. Castle flew patrols during the Battle of the Somme, taking many aerial photographs and, writing about one of his flights, described how he was just about to go on patrol and had already started the engine of his aeroplane when he suddenly realized that he was not wearing his prayer chain round his neck:

> Of course I am far too superstitious to go up without it, so I stopped my engine, got out of my machine, and went to my hut where I found it. I was too bundled up and had no time to undress, so I tied it round my wrist. Well, got up in the air about 10,000 feet when I spotted four Huns. Then I was glad I had gone back for my prayer, because I thought to myself 'Here's where I get it'.[41]

A dogfight ensued and Castle survived. He served on the Western Front for nine months following which he was sent to Fort Worth, Texas, as a flight training instructor for the Royal Flying Corps. Castle was killed on 15 February 1918 during a training flight which crashed as he attempted to avoid another aeroplane.

A thumb-size copy of the 91st Psalm accompanied pilot Robert Loraine when flying:[42]

> He that dwelleth in the secret place of the most High shall abide under the shadow of the Almighty... Thou shalt not be afraid for the terror by night; nor for the arrow that flieth by day;... A thousand shall fall at thy side, and ten thousand at thy right hand; but it shall not come nigh thee... There shall be no evil befall thee... With long life I will satisfy him, and shew him my salvation.[43]

The 91st Psalm is known as the psalm of protection and Loraine carried it in his breast pocket, thereby testifying to his attitude towards spirituality and well-being. It is not known where his copy of the psalm came from. Australian pilot Geoffrey Wall wrote in a letter that he 'rapidly recited the 91st Psalm (as mother advises)' for a positive outcome.[44]

Some people saw the war as an opportunity to cheat people and make money. The *Daily Mail* newspaper ran a series of articles in January 1917 exposing such a person, named F. Rawson, who claimed that his magic could 'allay the sufferings of the wounded, the perils of the missing'.[45] Rawson's 'magic' was in the form of being paid to say a long-distant prayer for a loved one. Thus, we have the situation that, if people *pay* for good fortune, then more potency is attributed to it. In an attempt to accumulate monetary fortune, Rawson also decreed that servicemen would be afforded protection if they carried a copy of the 91st Psalm.[46] Airmen and soldiers were prepared to 'believe' in such newly made-up claims that had no rational founding whatsoever. Christian religion and superstition/folklore were seemingly mingled together in an attempt to grasp at means of increasing chances of survival.

It is possible that people were becoming disillusioned with religion as they sought mystical protection elsewhere. Indeed, Annette Becker relates how servicemen relied on superstition to get them through the First World War. She reports how researchers came together during the war – French and Italian priests, anthropologists and classical historians – to try to understand superstitious practices and describes prayers which pre-dated the war that were revived during the war:

> Prayer to protect against firearms. As a counter-charm, recite this prayer three times in succession every morning before breakfast,

wear it and you will be preserved from all peril and danger of death, and you will always overcome your enemies.

 Prayer: Eccé, Crucem, domini, fugité, partès, adverse, vicis, l'eodé, Tribu, Juda, make the sign of the cross, radix, clavo.[47]

People believed that superstition and religion would provide greater survival odds as they hedged their bets. Belief in both religion and magic was turned to in order to achieve the same thing, that is to survive the war. Aviators believed in religion. Aviators believed in superstition. They seemingly combined both. Indeed, 'two men may behave in exactly the same way, and yet one of them may be religious and the other not'.[48]

Belief, Action, and Objects

We have seen how aviators' superstitions manifested themselves in physical reality in terms of bodily ritual and the use of material culture as lucky mascots. First World War aviators were in touch with their world through their emotions as they engaged with their material air world, sometimes in very individual and creative ways. The use of lucky mascots was driven by an aviator's instinct to survive and they relied on, and, to some extent, were controlled by, lucky mascots, superstition, and ritual to create a world they imagined they could control.

 Since emotions are cultural, they are predisposed to archaeological study for they are 'historically specific and experientially embodied', and, therefore, a significant means of enriching the archaeological and anthropological interpretation of the experiences of a First World War aviator.[49] Such belief in superstition is a dimension of an aviator's social existence that should be considered within the context of culture.

 By categorizing the mascots carried by First World War airmen we further our understanding of the relationships between men and objects.

 Things are never magical by themselves for they require the intervention of human intentions. The aviator in receipt of a mascot as a gift and who subsequently carries it, wears it, or attaches it to his aeroplane, is sending a message to his social world – he is perhaps not so confident in his own flying skills that he would not accept help from a lucky mascot.

 No less than 39 per cent of the sample of mascots studied here came from Category F – personal objects infused with special/intimate meaning personal to the aviator. Such items were either owned by the pilot or an item endowed with personal meaning, perhaps memories, and given to the pilot for luck.

 Lucky mascots, particularly with a religious connection such as a prayer or a Bible, often became part of the body worn next to the skin, as if it had to touch the aviator's living body, adjacent to his beating heart, for it to be effective. Indeed, if we consider it an extension of the body, we deconstruct the Cartesian distinction between self and other or person and thing. Such objects signified intense personal attachment and a heightened sense of intimacy and which 'embodied, bridged and transformed the material, social and imagined worlds' of First World War pilots.[50] French sociologist Marcel Mauss believed that the first human artefact is the human body itself, and that action by and upon the body is the core to understanding culture.[51] Whilst objects may be considered extensions of the human body, the body itself may also be considered as a 'thing' to adorn in order to relay a message to and about one's social world. In fact, it can be argued that it is the merging of such adornments and the body that create the entity of the 'social body'. However, it is acknowledged that the social body/display body focusing on identity was already present in the distinctive RFC uniform and paraphernalia marking pilots out as a class apart – before any mascot is even considered.

Some 15 per cent of the research sample suggests that aviators' lucky mascots were associated with good luck in traditional folklore which then transformed into a folklore of flying. The aviators could be seen as preserving and/or adapting superstitious customs and popular beliefs as folklore and ethnic heritage. This has parallels with the anthropologist Bronislaw Malinowski's famous work on the relationship between myth and magic amongst the Trobriand islanders of Melanesian New Guinea. Myth and magic were an everyday necessity for the Trobrianders, accompanying all practical activities, and forming an integral part of their culture. Malinowski regarded myths as part of human experience and the essence of social life. These myths provided practical rules for the performance of ritual and of technical aspects of life, and for the Trobriand islanders, were used in their boat-building activities. In one sense it can be suggested that there is an analogy between the wooden fishing canoes of the Trobrianders and a First World War wooden aircraft. The canoes were decorated with the carving and painting talents of the Trobrianders and infused with their hopes and fears, and that their knowledge and skill would ensure that the built canoe would be stable and swift. First World War aviators similarly decorated their aircraft and embodied their own fears and anxieties in their technologies via ritual behaviour. This can be compared to ritual behaviour by First World War pilots flying in contested air space when fear and anxiety were ever present. Indeed, magic put 'order and sequence' into the various activities undertaken by Malinowski's Trobrianders and it inspired them with confidence as it did for First World War aviators.[52]

The life expectancy of a First World War pilot in 1916 was three weeks on average.[53] In 1917, the life expectancy of a First World War aviator from posting until death was just eleven days.[54] Pilots knew this beforehand and such information would have added considerably to their fears and anxieties. In addition, there were many fatalities in training particularly in take-off and landing. The aeroplanes were fragile and could break up in flight without warning, adding to the perceived dangers. Thus, the particular circumstances of First World War combat flying exaggerated their need for mascots.

Aviators' belief in luck and superstition stemmed from folklore published in newspapers, magazines, and journals that were popular during the First World War. Such contemporary texts are important primary evidence. They provide a context for understanding that people engaged with objects not because of their form and function but through a gift economy as explored by Marcel Mauss where the significance of gifting a lucky mascot highlighted the relationship between the giver and the receiver (aviator).[55] Mauss' phenomenological approach to gift exchange informs the obligation involved in the act of giving, that is an aviator receiving a lucky mascot must, in return, endeavour to survive the war – not least, in this context, by practice flying sessions to hone their skills. In addition, it could be suggested that, if the pilot who had received the lucky mascot was killed, his sacrifice could be deemed to be his ultimate gift, such reciprocity revealing the social cycle of gift giving.

Society regarded such deaths to be a sacrifice as the Cross of Sacrifice in all Commonwealth War Graves Commission (CWGC) cemeteries containing forty-plus burials attests. After the war it was widely considered a duty to visit the graves as a reciprocal act of remembrance, such gift cycles engaging people in a deeply felt commitment. This is significant in that it broadens social relations and obligations. However, a gift may not only be reciprocal for there exists a variety of possible responses at different levels and there might be many such responses at any one time. For example:

(a) the object could be a personal gift from, for example, a girlfriend or wife. The aviator could purchase an item and send it back home in return;
(b) an aviator could give his wife, mother, or girlfriend a trophy from a downed aeroplane – this is a different and visceral level of reciprocation, real war material from a real conflict;
(c) the wife, mother, or girlfriend may receive a postcard borded in black informing her that the pilot is lost in action or killed. Did he give his life for her? Many felt that way in a complex mix of emotion – grief, gratitude, and longing.

The loved one gives the lucky mascot regardless of these three levels. Ultimately, the aviator contributes to the winning of the war so becomes a small part of national victory and thus contributes to the gift of peace – signifying that not all gifts are tangible objects.

Friends and relatives of aviators gave them mascots for protection through the 'agency' of belief – in that these young airmen and their relatives displayed a half-belief in luck, fate, and providence. Folklore explanations concerning magic that were current during the early twentieth century can be deployed to aid our understanding of these issues arguably far better than endless academic debate on theory.[56]

Many aviators relied on objects such as lucky charms or believed in omens and rituals to create 'an imagined structure of security, sense and control' in their environment.[57] Anxious over the uncertainty of the time they would die, pilots created innovative means in an attempt to attract good fortune, looking upon certain objects and incidents as good or bad omens. The pilot's body became a microcosm of the wider world of belief in propitious directions.

Chapter 8

Trench-art Propeller Grave Markers and the Stories they Tell

The following quotation is evocative of early aviation:

> A mechanic swung the propeller and the engine coughed, fired and spluttered again; then someone behind me yelled 'Contact' and the propeller melted into a blue mist in front of me.[1]

Propellers of First World War aeroplanes were made from wood, often mahogany, and their unique shapes are characteristic of a period lasting about fifteen years, from December 1903 when the Wright brothers first flew at Kittyhawk, North Carolina, to the end of the First World War in November 1918.

In this chapter I investigate wooden aeroplane propellers retrieved from crashed aircraft and reworked into trench-art propeller grave markers for aviators' graves. Pilot Duncan Grinnell-Milne observed, '[w]here's poor old P buried? We ought to stick a propeller-cross over his grave. A damn good fellow.'[2]

Taking a 'biographical approach' this chapter identifies the events in the 'social life' of these distinctive objects through combing the literature to identify common events. Such markers may be considered 'in terms of their involvement in the expression and the creation of emotional relationships' and, since 'emotions are culturally constructed . . . they are amenable to archaeological [and anthropological] analysis'.[3] My aim is to reveal how the grave markers became imbued with pilots' flying experiences, and how new memorial spaces were created when these propellers were moved post-war to, for example, churchyards and private gardens. Adopting Hallam and Hockey's phrase 'spatialised memory', we see how these new spaces became powerful symbols of loss and memory and perhaps a living reminder of a loved one.[4]

This aspect of my investigation reveals (and in some ways creates) ever closer relationships between anthropology and archaeology through its shared focus on material culture and on human-object interaction. Individual stories attached to 'acquisition events' – the appropriation of the propeller, usually removed from a crashed aeroplane – bestow significance on the commemorative legacies and give the deceased a powerful presence today.

Before the standardized Portland stone headstones of the Imperial (now Commonwealth) War Graves Commission were erected, graves were marked by simple wooden crosses bearing a metal plate with an identifying inscription or, in some instances, for aviators of the RFC, a propeller grave marker.[5] Very few of these have withstood the test of time and it is mainly photographic and textual evidence that attest to their existence.

Life Events of a Propeller Grave Marker

From being the mechanism which allowed the aeroplane to fly, the propeller was recycled with emotional potency as a grave marker when the aircraft crashed. The social life of the propeller grave marker is differentially significant to those who act in and around it, such as the bereaved relatives and RFC colleagues. In seeking to understand how these distinctive grave markers became invested with meaning, I identified seven key events (Table 2), or social interactions. Such a 'cultural biography' approach to propeller grave markers afforded their stories new depth and dimension.[6]

Table 2: Events of Social Interaction in the Social Life of a Propeller Grave Marker

Event of Social Interaction Identified from Research of the Literature	Comments
A. Pre-acquisition event	The story of the aviator's death apportions value, meaning, and significance to the propeller grave marker, as well as being representative of other grave markers.
B. Acquisition event	The appropriation of the propeller, usually removed from a crashed aeroplane; sometimes the propeller from the deceased's aeroplane was used to make the grave marker, but not always.
C. Manufacture event	The propeller was crafted into a grave marker, usually by a skilled person, who would have the requisite tools to hand, e.g. the squadron carpenter, rigger, or armourer. Once reworked, it also becomes a trench-art memorial.
D. Erection event and funeral	Propeller is erected over the grave, usually by RFC colleagues. Funeral possible, but not always.

Event of Social Interaction Identified from Research of the Literature	Comments
E. Post-war visitation event	Visits by, for example, a family member on a personal visit or as part of an organized pilgrim tour; a representative from a group such as the Salvation Army in the event that a relative was unable to visit; a returning serviceman. Such visits of the bereaved fuelled the trade of souvenir trench art as civilians scoured the battlefields for the war materiel necessary to make souvenirs for the pilgrim tourists to purchase.
F. Lost or destroyed event	Propeller grave marker was removed from the grave to be replaced by the uniform headstones erected by the CWGC after the war. If the propeller grave marker was not destroyed by the CWGC, it might have been transported to the UK, usually by a relative, to, for example, a private garden, church, or churchyard.
G. Donation elsewhere event	There are instances of propeller grave markers being donated to a museum to become an exhibit behind the window of a glass cabinet, and donated to Salisbury Cathedral too.

These events impart new layers of meaning to the propeller grave marker for they invest them with significance and meaning in terms of immersive social interactions before the biplane crashed and how we experience them today.

Although a cultural biography approach was integral to my identification of these seven events, I have also drawn on first-hand evidence from aviators' diaries, letters, books, and photographs. In doing so, it is possible, in affording another dimension, to give these and the objects discussed in the following two chapters a voice. In this way, the propeller grave marker becomes a repository for an aviator's conflict flying experiences – such as those described in Chapters 3 and 4. As such, it is the story of both the aviator's death (the pre-acquisition event) and how the propeller came to be acquired, for example by 'souveniring' (acquisition event) and the grave marker's subsequent manufacture event that contributes to the overall value, meaning, and significance of the object as a commemorative legacy.[7]

Propeller Grave Markers as Trench Art, the Pre-acquisition Event

Australian John Hay travelled to England to learn to fly, gaining his Royal AeroClub Aviators Certificate (No. 3039) on 2 June 1916. He then enlisted in the RFC, travelling to France in August 1916, as a scout pilot with No. 40 Squadron which was equipped with FE 8 pusher biplanes, that is the engine was at the rear of the aeroplane.[8] On 23 January 1917, whilst flying FE 8 number 6388 on patrol, Hay shot down two German aeroplanes. He was later attacked by a group of five enemy aircraft from Jasta 11 before becoming the seventeenth victim of Richthofen.[9] Lieutenant Hay's aeroplane caught fire and he was witnessed jumping from a burning aeroplane to his death. His body was subsequently recovered by Canadian troops.[10] Fellow officers had a memorial plaque engraved that was attached to the propeller grave marker from his aeroplane that read: 'The earth holds not a braver gentleman'.[11] The plaque in the photograph (see Plate 10) was initially placed on a propeller grave marker (see Figure 13), that had been erected over Hay's grave and was subsequently given to his family and brought back to Australia.[12]

Figure 13. *The propeller grave marker of 2nd Lieutenant John Hay, 40 Squadron, RFC, Aire Communal Cemetery, France (Accession No. P02118.002).* (Courtesy Australian War Memorial)

The Canadian servicemen who buried Hay also arranged for a piece of tin to be cut into the shape of a ribbon with the words '*à notre frère*' (our brother) painted on the front in pale blue as a mark of respect (see Plate 11). The significance of including John Hay's death here is the manner of his death. RFC and RNAS pilots did not have parachutes that would enable them to bail out in an emergency in an attempt to save their lives, although they had been invented. Fighter pilot Sholto Douglas wrote:

> On one patrol early in 1917 I was flying in formation, and I saw that the observer, poor devil, was standing up in the back seat agitatedly trying to call to the attention of his pilot, a glint of flame that was just starting to appear along the side of their aircraft. A moment later there was a violent explosion and the whole aircraft disintegrated. Such a sight was all too common in our flying of those days, and so far as I was concerned it was one of the most horrible that one could witness.[13]

Observers in balloons, on the other hand, *were* supplied with parachutes but their bulkiness would not fit into the cramped cockpits of biplanes. Sholto Douglas wrote that a parachute would have enabled pilots to escape from damaged aeroplanes thus avoiding an awful death and just that thought alone would have been good for morale. Later in life, Sholto:

> . . . learnt to my disgust that the reason why we did not have [parachutes] was an astonishing policy adopted during the First World War that deliberately denied us the use of parachutes . . .
>
> When I learnt about that, I thought about what we had to endure and I recalled how so many men had died in such agony – all because somebody had thought so little of us that they believed that providing us with parachutes would encourage us to abandon our aircraft . . . It was indeed a 'disgraceful' reason for arriving at such a contemptible decision.[14]

The High Command refused to provide pilots with parachutes and their absence became a point of contention that is still debated today.[15] Some German pilots did have parachutes and Lieutenant Colonel Strange remembers that:

> In 1930, met about 50 German pilots and renewed his friendship with Bolle. Met . . . several members of Richthofen's famous Squadron, including Ernst Udet . . . a strange mixture of caution

Plate 1. *A popular postcard. Many postcards depicting a sense of humour were sent during the First World War.* (Author's collection)

Above left: Plate 2. *A postcard from the Fum's Up! set, Oilette Series Postcard No. 8792A. This postcard is entitled 'The Optimist'. First date used 28 June 1915.* (Author's collection)

Above right: Plate 3. *Sterling silver Fum's Up! Charm, circa 1914. The arms are articulated, whilst the head is made from wood and the eyes are genuine pink rubies. A four-leaf clover imprint is visible on the forehead and the back of the head is marked with the words 'Touch Wud'. It was considered a very lucky charm. Dimensions: 31mm x 10mm.* (© Author)

Plate 4. *Examples of Nénette, Rintintin, and a baby. Crafted from white and pale-pink wool, joined together with a length of wool. Dimensions: height: 50mm; width: 30mm.* (© IWM (EPH 004664))

Plate 5. *RFC pilot charm presented as trench art, constructed in the image of a Handley Page O/400 aeroplane.* (© Author)

Right: Plate 6. *Sunny Jim.* (© Gerry Crutchley)

Below left: Plate 7. *The front side of a First World War USAAS pilot's religious charm. Made from sterling silver with small enamelled areas in red and white representing the USAAS pilot wings. The charm depicts St Christopher above the pilot wings.* (© Author)

Below right: Plate 8. *The rear side of a First World War USAAS pilot's religious charm.* (© Author)

Above: Plate 9. *A 3-D model of a monoplane made from gold-coloured metal, produced in 1916.* (© IWM (EPH 3471))

Left: Plate 10. *A rounded brass plaque with a pair of pilot's brevets engraved at the top. The plaque had been attached to the propeller grave marker of 2nd Lieutenant John Hay, No. 40 Squadron, RFC (Accession No. REL23683).* (© and courtesy Australian War Memorial)

Below: Plate 11. *A fragment of tin funeral wreath plaque, 2nd Lieutenant John Hay, No. 40 Squadron, RFC (Accession No. REL34599).* (©Australian War Memorial)

Plate 12. *A row of four RFC graves, Terlincthun British cemetery, Wimille, France.* (© Author)

Plate 13. *A trench-art biplane with twin propeller blades, stamped 'Ypres'. Souvenir of the First World War.* (© Author)

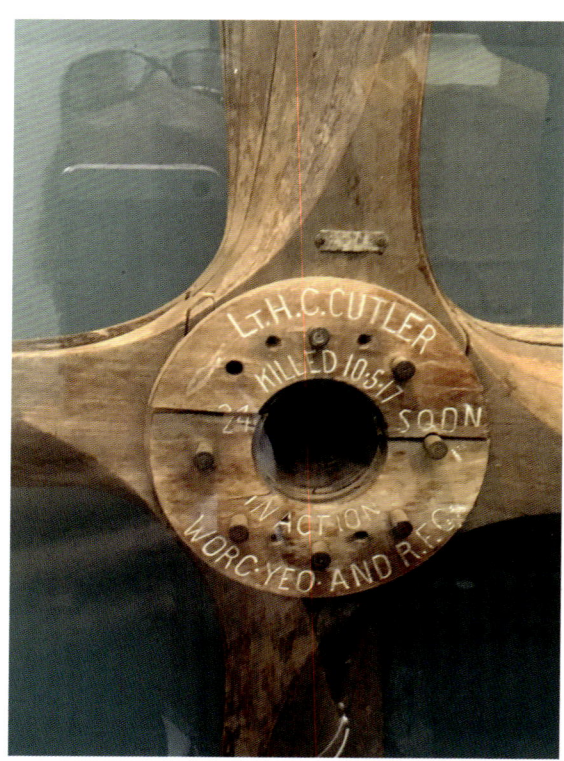

Above left: Plate 14. *The propeller grave marker of Lieutenant Herbert Cecil Cutler.* (© Author, courtesy Museum of the Worcestershire Yeomanry)

Above right: Plate 15. *A section of a wooden propeller blade with a painted scene depicting an RFC aeroplane flying through anti-aircraft explosions. Dimensions: length: 45cm x width bottom: 20cm; width: top 15cm.* (IWM (EPH 9961))

Left: Plate 16. *A trench-art-style photograph frame with photographs of an unknown serviceman and his friends and family, made from the wooden propeller tip of a First World War aeroplane. Dimensions: length: 44cm; bottom width: 22cm; top width: 6cm.* (© Author)

Plate 17. *A trench-art propeller clock from the archive stores of the Shuttleworth Collection. Provenance unknown.* (© Author, courtesy Shuttleworth Collection)

Plate 18. *A trench-art model of a biplane with a four-bladed propeller. Dimensions: width: circa 16cm.* (© Author, courtesy Shuttleworth Collection)

Plate 19. *A trench-art model of a biplane with a two-bladed propeller. Dimensions: width: circa 16cm.* (© Author, courtesy Shuttleworth Collection)

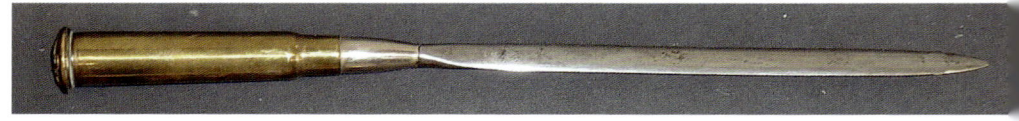

Plate 20. *A trench-art letter opener.* (© Author)

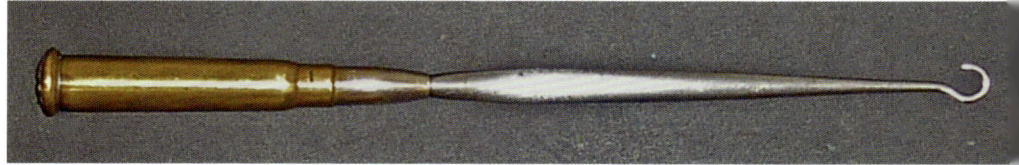

Plate 21. *A trench-art button hook.* (© Author)

Plate 22. *An RFC button, used to personalize the trench-art letter opener and button hook.* (© Author)

and daredevil – which is, I suppose, what every airman ought to be; he was one of the few who wore a parachute during the war, and told me that it saved his life twice.[16]

Indeed, two days before the end of the war, Sholto Douglas witnessed a German pilot escape from his burning aeroplane, 'I saw to my astonishment, a little pink parachute open out. The pilot was attached to it, and he was floating safely down to earth'.[17]

Aviators' diaries, letters, and books reveal that the absence of a parachute caused considerable anger. Pilots dreaded the thought of dying in a flaming aeroplane. RFC ace Mick Mannock, after witnessing one of his victims going down in flames, wrote in his diary: 'It was a horrible sight and made me feel sick'.[18] Mannock was known to carry his service revolver with him whilst flying as he would prefer to shoot himself rather than die in a flaming aeroplane.[19] Mannock died in a flaming aeroplane on 20 July 1917, although it is not known whether he managed to shoot himself.

Acquisition

Duncan Grinnell-Milne wrote that in a BE aeroplane it was impossible to fire straight forward because the propeller got in the way and evasive means had to be adopted to avoid hitting the propellers:[20]

> The forward gun-mounting gave an arc on either bow, above and below, but to fire straight ahead would be to send shots into the propeller, possibly smashing a blade and consequently bringing the machine down. To hit our enemy, we had to turn slightly away from him, put in a burst or two and turn back quickly so as not to open the range.[21]

Even undertaking such evasive action, propellers were hit by gunfire and aeroplanes crashed which meant that pieces of wooden propellers were readily available to be 'souvenired' and/or recycled into trench-art/propeller grave markers (see Figure 14). This letter opener has been made from scrap metal from an aeroplane (probably the steel struts) that has been attached to a wooden handle crafted from a piece of wood from an aeroplane propeller. The wooden handle appears to be in the shape of the handle of a pistol and, on holding it myself, it rests very neatly in the hand but I feel that this particular letter opener would not be an easy object to manoeuvre to open a letter. The small piece of wooden propeller would have been readily available and may even have been an offcut from one of the many propeller grave markers that were made by a squadron carpenter or armourer.

82   The Archaeology of the Royal Flying Corps

Figure 14. *A trench-art letter opener crafted from the wooden propeller and engine strut of a Sopwith Pup aeroplane. Dimensions: length: circa 20cm (Accession No. 96/3).* (© Author, courtesy Shuttleworth collection)

Figure 15. *A crashed German biplane with 'souveniring' Tommies, note whilst the propeller is still in place, the aeroplane linen has already been souvenired.* (Author's collection)

Crashed aeroplanes were deemed good for general 'souveniring' beyond propellers – for example, wing and tail linen (see Figure 15).

So fragile were the aeroplanes, that it did not take much to damage them. War artist Major Sir William Orpen wrote of an occasion on the Western Front when he watched novice English pilots perform aeroplane trials:

> I remember one poor chap in particular. He circled the aerodrome 12 times, each time coming down for landing and each time funking it at the last moment. At last he did land, two or three bumps, and then – apparently slowly – the machine's nose went to the ground and gracefully it turned turtle . . . The thing that amazed me was, that

...ot down by Lieutenant Anthony John
...he two-bladed propeller can clearly

...ently, the damage to it was
...mashed to bits.[22]

...ha aeroplane was shot down by
...er Private A.T.C. Stagg, whilst
...Fighter 4636 (see Figure 16). On
...Arkell wrote about the propeller
...ng to retrieve it as a souvenir.[23]
...propellers to be appropriated.

...arker represents the creator's
...airman's. The propellers were a
...with the deceased's rank, name,
...e RFC or the RAF, and perhaps,

Figure 17. *The propeller grave marker of Lieutenant W. H. Ryder. The grave marker is now situated inside St Peter's Church, Little Thurlow, Suffolk.* (© Author)

means of death, for example, 'killed in action' or 'killed in flying accident' (Figure 17). The date of death was important for it related to the last experience of the deceased.

The propeller grave marker is imbued with time because of its 'manufacturing event'. Somebody, possibly the squadron carpenter or rigger, devoted their time to cut the propeller down on three sides to form the appearance of a cross, the longer upright length being easier to bury into the ground for support. Time was also invested in engraving the deceased's name and date of death onto the centre of the propeller, thereby marking the aviator's presence in historical and geographical space and time. Perhaps the engraver may have been in a hurry, making a mistake in the carving of the name that he would then have to rectify, for example, on the propeller grave marker of Lieutenant Cutler, the name 'Cutler' was initially misspelt on the carving of the letter 'L', having to be re-carved from the letter 'E'. In a sense, of course, the re-working of the propeller makes it a trench-art memorial as well – enhanced by its status as a metonym for the whole aeroplane, and a metaphor for all dead aviators' grave markers, inasmuch as it may not have been his propeller – and so the symbolism becomes generic.

Erection and Funeral

Erecting a propeller grave marker was a very personal occasion with colleagues of the deceased airman taking the time and effort to individualize his grave, doing their duty and ensuring it was worthy of him. Cecil Lewis remembers: 'The graves had been dug, and the Padre conducted the short ceremony at the graveside. The riggers had made crosses from four-bladed props, cutting off three blades short and leaving one long, and embossed their names on copper plates, covering the hubs where the bolt went through.'[24]

The size of the propeller grave marker immediately draws one's gaze, directing attention, for it has become a focal point in the cemetery. It visually identifies the burial of a member of the RFC and such burials became a common sight on the First World War landscape. Once such distinctive and visually salient grave markers had been erected they became symbolic objects, attracting a gathering of people, visually informing them of the death of a First World War aviator and communicating the way they should feel in terms of emotion – an example of an object making people learn how to act appropriately at a funeral.[25] Propeller grave markers became 'social actors' – they were not something just to be viewed, they were integral to human action. The life of these propeller grave markers is thus significant to bereaved relatives and aviators of the RFC.

Brigadier General Gordon Shephard gained his Royal Aero Club Certificate No. 215 on 14 May 1912 and subsequently joined the RFC. When the war began, he flew to France with the first five squadrons on 13 August 1914.[26] He died in an aeroplane accident in France on 19 January 1918 whilst flying his Nieuport Scout, B3610. A propeller grave marker was erected over his burial (see Figure 18).[27] The photograph reveals that the propeller grave marker lay in a cemetery full of small wooden crosses and that there were other propeller grave markers present – a somewhat surreal earthly image commemorating violent death in the air.

On Brigadier General Shephard's death, Major Hughes-Hallett of the Royal Artillery, recalled their flights together and wrote to Shephard's mother. In particular he described an uneventful flight which nevertheless impressed itself on both their minds as they returned from reconnaissance over Lille during which they had been unable to discover any hostile movement because of low-level cloud. He related how they flew for several miles just above the cloud bank as though in another world, and as if they:

> . . . [w]ere in some fairy skiff skimming over some fairy sea. There was a glorious sunshine about, no grand or disturbing masses of cloud to spoil the enchantment, and a few feet below came the vast level surface of this endless sea. We both felt a little dazed, I think, by the absolute quiet and complete detachment from a petty world we had heard of somewhere beneath us, but with which we calm beings had but little connection.[28]

He went on to impart that it was a dangerous trip because of the risk that an enemy aeroplane might fly up through the cloud to discover them, but, for the whole 2-hour flight they were fortunate in that they did not see another aeroplane, and:

> nothing would have induced us to miss the sense of peace and detachment . . .
>
> The descent into the gloom and drizzle of petty squabbles was one of the saddest things I ever remember. I have written of this

Figure 18. *The propeller grave marker of Brigadier General Gordon Shephard, with flower wreath from I Brigade.* (Author's collection)

uneventful journey because we both felt the deep impression it gave, and even now at moments in my mind it is more fresh than any incident of the war.[29]

This is an emotive piece of prose and tells clearly of their feelings, thoughts, and opinions of the war. Comrades of the First World War dead were concerned with sparing the feelings of loved ones at home. In writing this letter in this manner, Hughes-Hallett is understandably trying to spare the mother's feelings, thus controlling her emotional proximity to the event and screening her from the horror of her son's death.

Not all dead servicemen were given funerals. However, a high-ranking pilot such as Brigadier General Shephard was accorded a burial with full military honours with some 20 generals and 1,000 officers in attendance. The burial was a sensorial event for it was preceded by Canadian pipers and a firing party, the noise echoing around the countryside for all to hear. There were numerous spoken eulogies and remembrances, a lone voice speaking clearly for all attendees to hear and focus on.

Air Marshal Sir Hugh Trenchard wrote in a letter to Lord and Lady Shephard:

> His work in the first part of the war made him . . . one of the pioneers of artillery work, that is observing from the air for artillery fire . . . He also worked very hard at the co-operation of low-flying machines with infantry, and in no small measure the success of this type of Flying Corps work was due to some of his suggestions.[30]

This informs us how Brigadier General Shephard flew and the propeller grave marker is therefore representative of his skilled and sentient knowledge of flying. When, for example, he observed from the air for artillery fire and successfully directed the ranging of the guns, he became the eyes of the army as he enabled those manning heavy guns on the ground to see beyond their immediate horizon, thus extending the active battlefield and creating a new killing zone.

Both Allied and German pilots displayed a great mutual respect for each other, especially when pilots crashed and died over enemy lines. An example of where Germans did the same for a British pilot is described by Edwin Campion Vaughan, a British officer serving in the Royal Warwickshire Regiment. Situated amongst some German graves were the graves of three British airmen. Each grave was marked with a wooden cross erected by the Germans detailing their ages, squadrons, and date of death. Their broken aeroplane propellers were left at the foot of their graves.[31]

In a letter to his mother, Captain F. Williams MC, DFC wrote:

> One thing I will say for the enemy they have some jolly stout fellows amongst them and when it comes to burying our dead they always do it nicely and put over the graves 'Brave English Soldiers who died for their Fatherland in the fighting by Ypres July 1915' for example and what more glorious thing could be written over one's grave than *'Tapfer Englisher Flieger… Kampf gefallen'* ('brave English airman … killed in action').[32]

Lieutenant Denys Corbett Wilson survived ten months in the Royal Flying Corps before being shot down with his observer, 2nd Lieutenant Isaac Newton Woodiwiss, on 10 May 1915. They were killed by a shell whilst undertaking a reconnaissance over German lines. A German aviator dropped a message over British lines to say that the men were both killed instantly and were being buried at a cemetery at Fourne, France – within German lines.[33] The bodies of both men were exhumed and reburied side-by-side in the British cemetery at Cabaret-Rouge, Souchez, France.[34] A degree of mutual admiration and respect seemed to develop between the two air forces, even visiting each other in hospital:

> [after enduring a dogfight with two German Albatros fighters] . . . our front Lewis gun jammed . . . the two Albatros were attacking from opposite directions, . . . watched one of them crash land.
> . . . was given the windmill-type speed indicator from the Albatros . . . The pilot of the Albatros was Ltn Josef Flintz of Jasta 18. I looked in and saw him in Baillieul Hospital next day and gave him a hundred cigarettes.[35]

Thus we see how both the 'community of pilots', regardless of nationality, and the ability of the propeller grave markers transcend the division between friend and foe, and thus become a transnational symbolic object.

Post-war Visitation

Returning to the Western Front after the war, ex-soldier Henry Williamson recalls walking behind what would have been the German lines and coming across the solitary grave of an un-named British airman that had a propeller for a grave marker 'with pansies and mignonette for coverlet, railed off from the cattle around the resting place of the "brave, unknown English airman who fell in battle, July 14, 1916"'.[36] Many of the bereaved travelled to the Western Front to find the graves of their dead relatives or, in the absence of a body, to visit one of the many memorials erected to the missing. Such visits were emotional and tactile events. It may have been that the bereaved wanted to see the name on the propeller grave marker, headstone, or memorial. The visitors took photographs of the names and, sometimes, kissed the letters of the carved name of a loved one or the actual headstone or grave marker. Many of the visitors came equipped with tracing paper and pencil to trace the name of their dead relative.[37] Evidently the materialized name on the headstone or memorial was of paramount importance not least because it was a final tangible connection with the deceased and was enough to bring forth feelings of emotion and sentiment.

Visitors left gifts at the grave or memorial, including flowers from their own gardens, or wreaths, bestowing a 'shrine-like quality' as the graveside became 'a focus of devotion and physical contact between the dead and the living'.[38] They returned home with mementoes from the grave, including headstone moulds, seeds from the plants growing by the headstone, or stones from the grave itself. Such souvenirs enabled the bereaved to bring home 'a tangible link with the memory, or even the spirit of the dead'.[39] Perhaps such souvenirs, appropriated from the immediate vicinity of the grave, could be perceived to be a gift from the dead.

Lieutenant Guy Ashwin was killed in action; he crashed through his aeroplane which broke up whilst flying at 2,000ft. In September 1914, aged 17½ years, Ashwin joined the London Regiment. In January 1915, he was posted to France and fought in several ground battles and was wounded twice. In February 1917, he returned to England to join the RFC, and, on receiving his commission, he returned to the Western Front. He was killed alongside his observer and is buried in the Aubigny Extension Cemetery, near Arras.[40] A propeller grave marker was placed over his grave, though later removed. The Salvation Army organized a war graves visiting programme, and its members accompanied relatives to the Western Front. In the event that relatives were unable to travel, the Salvation Army arranged for flowers to be placed on the grave and a photograph taken, placed in a card alongside pressed flowers, and posted to the relative. It is known that a member of the Salvation Army visited the grave of Lieutenant Ashwin.[41] The propeller grave marker, secured in an upright position on a plinth of wood, towered over the small wooden crosses that filled the cemetery. The propeller marks the significance of the way Lieutenant Ashwin died and, if it is the propeller rescued from his own crashed aeroplane, it is infused with his sensorial flying experiences. If it is not the propeller from his crash, it is representative of his sensorial flying experiences.

Graham Seton Hutchison wrote a battlefield guide aimed at the thousands of people planning to make pilgrimages to France and Flanders to give them 'a full and fair view of the battlefields'. He advises that whilst 'photographs will assist imagination', they are unable 'to recall the voices of the night and the stench of gas mingled with that of rotting corpses'.[42] The pilgrim tourists may have visited the French town of Saint-Omer where the General Headquarters of the RFC was situated. Pulteney and Brice published a guide with a large pull-out map detailing landmarks, cemeteries, and memorials that had already been erected so tourists would know where to visit.[43]

German officer Ernst Jünger noted that 'the countryside was dotted about with the skeletal wreckages of downed aeroplanes, an indication that machines were playing an ever greater part on the battlefield'.[44] Indeed, for a brutal insight into the war, visitors may have visited the Aeroplane Cemetery in West-Vlaanderen, near Ypres, Belgium, so named from the wreck of an aeroplane which was, at the time, preserved near the present position of the Cross of Sacrifice.[45]

The crashed aeroplane became a reminder of the stark and brutal realities of what it means to sacrifice one's life for one's country, portraying the particularly emotional aspects of such sites of loss in modern conflict archaeology. Its replacement by the uniform CWGC grave would not include such experience for 'in every memorial, something has been left out or forgotten . . . the omission or exclusion of the pain and horror of war on those memorials'.[46] It is not known what happened to the crashed aeroplane but it is possible that it was souvenired or moved to a squadron's airfield (see Figure 19).

Figure 19. *A German scout aeroplane brought down over Allied lines, Western Front, France.* (Author's collection)

The bereaved may also have visited other aviation-related towns such as Arras as well as the graves of flying aces.[47] Table 3 below contains details of some of the cemeteries visited during my research that contain airmen's graves and would have been places of great interest to the bereaved visitors.

Table 3: Samples of Cemeteries in France and Belgium Containing the Graves of First World War Aviators, Visited by the Author in 2012

Cemetery	Number of First World War Graves	Comments
Lijssenthoek Military Cemetery, Belgium	10,121 overall 90 airmen's graves	Location of many casualty clearing stations, close to the front, but out of range of most German field artillery.
Longuenesse Souvenir Cemetery, Saint-Omer, France	3,397 overall 149 airmen's graves	Saint-Omer was the General Headquarters of the British Expeditionary Force from October 1914–March 1916. It was also the first port of call for many aviators arriving in France en route to their squadrons.
Poperinghe New Military Cemetery, Belgium	680 overall 4 airmen's graves	Poperinghe was the nearest town to Ypres that was considered reasonably safe.
Wavans British Cemetery, France	44 overall 12 airmen's graves	Flying ace Major James McCudden VC buried here.
Terlincthun British Cemetery, Wimille, France	3,762 overall 121 airmen's graves	There were many hospitals in the area. A bombing raid at Marquise in September 1918 caused the deaths of 46 RAF personnel. Plot IV, row C contains their graves (see Plate 12).
Boulogne Eastern Cemetery, St Martin, Boulogne, France	5,582 overall 12 airmen's graves	There were many hospitals in this area.
Étaples Military Cemetery, Nr Boulogne, France	11,435 overall 63 airmen's graves	Largest military cemetery in France. Built on the site of a former hospital. Unveiled 14 May 1922 by King George V.
Laventie Military Cemetery, La Gorgue, France	495 overall 5 airmen's graves	

Whilst we cannot physically experience the First World War, we can experience an artificial version of it through the landscapes offered to visitors on organized battlefield tours, and which Saunders calls 'commercially edited perceptions of reality'.[48] *Major and Mrs Holt's Battlefield Guide to the Somme*, for example, gives just such a version of the Somme landscape according to what they perceive visitors will find interesting and knowing that they do not have time to see everything; they point out important aviation-related towns such as Saint-Omer and Arras as well as graves of flying aces.[49] Battlefield tours run to schedules as to what can be fitted into a day as tourists stop for lunch and comfort breaks – an artificial landscape made especially for the gaze of tourists who 'authenticate' their experiences through the purchase of souvenirs.[50] Such a souvenir, however, is indicative of 'the second-hand experience of [a battlefield tourist]' and not of 'the lived experience of its maker' or originator.[51]

Post-war visitors often purchased civilian-made trench art, highlighting the entanglements between people and objects that materialize in such circumstances. As early as 1914, the *War Illustrated*, on a page entitled 'civilian curiosity in the evidences of war', printed photographs of civilian children and adults searching, in the Belgian countryside and northern France, for war-related souvenirs, collecting spent cartridge cases, bullets, and other objects as playthings and souvenirs of the fighting (see Figure 20).[52]

On the same page on which the abovementioned photograph was printed, the *War Illustrated* noted that '[s]ouvenir-hunting had become quite an industry where the fire of battle had raged' and it forecast with certainty that the 'traffic in war souvenirs will flourish in the years to come when the battlefields are the haunt of summer tourists'.[53] As civilians (men, women, and children) who had moved to safer areas during the war, returned to their towns and villages, they had to earn money to survive. Many cleared away the detritus from the war which was either

Figure 20. *Civilians hunting in the grass for German bullets and other souvenirs of the war, Senlis, northern France.* (Author's collection)

sold for scrap or became the raw material from which souvenir trench art could be made to sell to the battlefield pilgrims and visitors.⁵⁴ Would-be pilgrims were warned that 'metal debris is collected by the Belgians and dumps are generally noticed near the cottages. This is sold to the Government as scrap iron, so should not be rifled in the search for souvenirs'. Pulteney and Brice issued a warning to their readers 'against tampering with any shells or bombs they may come across, as serious accidents have occurred through the explosion of live ammunition'.⁵⁵ Such souvenirs therefore were contested objects. Indeed, Maurice Baring, in May 1917, recalls:

> Beverley, the HQ carpenter, blew up his hands by opening a bomb which someone had brought back as a souvenir. It was not his fault. He was told to do it. It has blown off three fingers and a thumb on one hand and his thumb from another. He was an admirable carpenter. It is most tragic, but it is to be hoped they may be able to make him artificial fingers at Roehampton.⁵⁶

Trench-art souvenir aeroplanes were made from the detritus of war and sold to battlefield visitors (see Plate 13). The model depicted here is characteristic of the Nieuport biplane, introduced in 1916, and flown by both the RFC and the French *Aéronautique Militaire* during the First World War. The fuselage of the model is constructed from a 7.92 x 57mm cartridge used by the French forces both in their carbines and in their Hotchkiss machine guns. The projectile is made from cupro-nickel with a lead core. The wheels of the model are the end caps of the same type of cartridge. The wings are made from brass sheet and the struts, propeller, and tail skid from copper rod and sheet – all readily available war materiel. The two-bladed propeller and the wheels are free-moving. The bottom wings move, whether by design, or not, is unclear, but they are only slotted into the side of the cartridge, although it is more likely that the soldering work has dissolved over time.

As with other non-aviation examples of post-war trench art, a clue to its date and function is given by the etched picture of the Menin Gate Memorial to the Missing under the name 'Ypres' on the commercially made plaque. Since the memorial was not unveiled until 24 July 1927, it is clear that souvenirs were being made by civilians well after the 1918 Armistice to take advantage of the battlefield tourists and pilgrims who visited France and Belgium. The souvenir biplane could possibly have been purchased by someone who had experienced the loss of a husband, brother, or son in the war, and/or whose name, perhaps, appears on the Menin Gate Memorial to the Missing.⁵⁷ The word 'Ypres' functions as a 'metonymic sign' for the model and may be considered as an actual piece of Ypres for the etched words become 'symbols in themselves' as they both 'transform and sacralise the [model] giving it a power it would not have without them'.⁵⁸

The power of these otherwise small models made from scrap is that they represent a miniature version of past events and a reminder of a post-war visit to the Western Front. Such souvenirs can be seen to 'possess a "sense of the sacred" which is underscored by an ambiguous tension between their associations with death and their continued life as memory-evoking objects for the living'.[59] It is ironic too that relatives visiting the area after the war, who purchased such a souvenir, took home an object made from the war materiel which had caused so much misery and suffering. The trench art biplane was probably not purchased by relatives of an aviator, but future generations may perhaps, mistakenly, think that the aeroplane indicated they had a relative who was a member of the RFC. The model is valuable because of its relation to the Western Front and may therefore be used to 'authenticate a past . . . experience'.[60]

As Alfred Gell observed, 'the smell of an object always *escapes*'.[61] Indeed, on receiving the model aeroplane, depicted in Plate 13, into my home, a smell of metal polish invaded the room, indicating, perhaps, that it had been recently polished by the seller from whom I had purchased it. This made me think back to the time it was brought home as a souvenir after a visit to Ypres and the Menin Gate and of it being polished by the subsequent owners periodically, almost ritually, before I acquired it. Indeed, the act of polishing prompted the polisher (the initial owner) to remember a lost loved one. The act of polishing represented a silent and emotional temporal communication linking the present with the past. In addition to being an object full of memories, such an object could be interpreted as possessing healing qualities as the bereaved had to come to terms with their grief. When I photographed the Ypres biplane, I polished it to make it camera ready. After only a couple of minutes, my forefinger and thumb were aching as a result of holding the Brasso-impregnated cloth too tightly as I polished trying to bring up a shine. My sense of tactility added to the palimpsest of previous owners' sensorial experiences in polishing the object and moving it through time.

Lost or Destroyed?

After the war, the CWGC dismantled the wooden crosses and propeller grave markers and gradually replaced them with the uniform Portland stone headstones we see today. Some visitors returned home with the wooden grave marker once the permanent headstone was in place as the CWGC offered the wooden crosses and propeller grave markers to relatives of the deceased on condition that the relative would arrange to ship them home; any remaining crosses and propellers were destroyed. They were often destroyed by burning in situ and the ashes were scattered across the burial ground or left in situ in the field for nature to absorb, a kind of second burial/cremation.[62]

Whereas propeller grave markers had immediately identified aviators' graves from a distance, the new uniform CWGC headstones did not, and visitors had to approach and peer closely to see the RFC crest and motto, *per ardua ad astra*, that now identified all aviators' graves.

Pulteney and Brice describe the new headstones for visiting pilgrims:

> Picture this strangely stirring place. A lawn enclosed of close-clipped turf, banded across with line on line of flowers, and linked by these bands of flowers, uncrowded, at stately intervals, stand in soldierly ranks the white headstones. And while they form as perfect, as orderly a whole as any regiment on parade, yet they do not shoulder each other. Every one is set apart in flowers, every one casts its shade upon a gracious space of green. Each one is stern in outline . . . for the crest of the regiment stands out with bold and arresting distinction above the strongly incised names.
> . . .
> It is filled with an atmosphere that leaves you very humble.[63]

If the propeller grave marker was not destroyed or lost it was transported elsewhere, usually by a relative. The original propeller grave marker that marked the grave of Captain Eric Horace Comber-Taylor RAF at the Esquelbecq Military Cemetery now resides inside St Peter's Church, Twineham, Sussex, being gifted to the church by his father in the 1920s.[64] Originally the propeller was kept outside this isolated ancient Sussex church, but being wood, and not protected from the elements, it did not weather well, so was moved inside the church to better preserve it. The propeller is engraved with Comber-Taylor's name, rank, RAF affiliation, date of death, and that he was killed in action. It also reads 'RIP' – rest in peace. Sometime after arriving at the church, an addition was made by securing it to a plain wooden cross with a small, pointed roof-like structure at the top. The following words were subsequently engraved on the wooden base: 'propeller cross from the grave of his son Eric Horace, Esquelbecq Military Cemetery'.

Removed from the ground at his burial in Esquelbecq, France, the base of the marker would have had soil from the Western Front landscape clinging to it. That soil would have been transported, along with the propeller grave marker, to its final location in England, connecting the memorial soils of both countries. A trail of memory is apparent as the propeller is connected to his grave in France; his memory exists simultaneously in two locations. People can visit his grave in France where his body is interred, or they can visit his propeller grave marker in England. The meaning, significance, and value of the propeller grave marker have altered, it no longer marks a grave – in its new location it marks the memory of Captain Eric Horace Comber-Taylor.

96   The Archaeology of the Royal Flying Corps

This propeller may be regarded as a sensorial object in that it is displayed openly in the church and, as church-goers and visitors to the church are visually drawn to it, they may be unable to resist the urge to touch and caress it. This created a 'patina of use-wear polish (caused by the wood literally absorbing [the] bodily secretions of sweat and oil' of church-goers and visitors.[65] The date of death signifies that it is connected to the First World War, and this may ignite a particular way of emotional feeling as people are drawn into a world beyond the church as they may think about that conflict, and the individual whose name is etched on the propeller.

The propeller, through viewing it, through touching it, may provoke the experience of a whole range of emotions and feelings. However, sight of the propeller may be regulated to times of church services. In this case, Sung Eucharist takes place every fourth Sunday from 10–11 am during which traditional and modern hymns are sung; and Sung Evensong every first Sunday from 6–7 pm during which time psalms and canticles are sung, thus placing this sentient object in an aural environment.[66] Also, red poppies and wreaths may be laid on or near the propeller at the customary annual Remembrance Sunday service as 'physicality, spirituality, symbolism and emotion link the living with the dead in a complex interplay of past and present'.[67] Placing the grave marker inside the church provides a space in the world where the viewer is reminded when and how to remember.

Donation Elsewhere

There was often a reason for donating propeller grave markers to particular museums. In the case of that dedicated to Lieutenant Herbert Cecil Cutler, it was given to the Museum of the Worcestershire Yeomanry because, before joining the RFC, he had served with the 2nd and 1st Queen's Own Worcestershire Hussars (the Worcester Yeomanry), a cavalry unit (see Plate 14). Figure 21 shows Cutler before he went to the Western Front.

Lieutenant Cutler transferred to the RFC, No. 24 Squadron, travelling to the Western Front on 21 March 1917 as a pilot, and was killed aged 26 on 10 May 1917, whilst flying a de Havilland DH2. His local newspaper, the *Bromsgrove, Droitwich and Redditch Weekly Messenger*, reported him as being killed in action, his death being a great shock to his father because, on the previous day, he had received letters from his son, written on the date of his death, describing how his aeroplane had been shot away but that he had had a very narrow escape.[68] He is buried in Templeux-le-Guerard British Cemetery, Somme, France.

The propeller grave marker, that originally marked Lieutenant Cutler's grave in France, was discovered in a garden in Bromsgrove, Worcestershire, believed

Trench-art Propeller Grave Markers and the Stories they Tell 97

Figure 21. *Lieutenant H.C. Cutler in his car in 1916, before he went to the Western Front.* (© and courtesy Museum of the Worcestershire Yeomanry)

to be that of his parents. Through Colonel Stamford Cartwright TD, who was then, coincidentally and somewhat poignantly, the Squadron Leader of one of the successor squadrons to the Queen's Own Worcestershire Hussars namely 67th (Queen's Own Warwickshire and Worcestershire Yeomanry) Signal Squadron near Bromsgrove, the grave marker was donated to the museum in 1982.[69]

The propeller grave marker displays .303 British military cartridges pushed through the mounting holes of the propeller, an additional embellishment of the creator and perhaps an acknowledgement of the fact that .303 ammunition was used in both Lewis and Vickers machine guns, both of which were employed as the main armament on British aircraft. In erecting the propeller grave marker dedicated to their son in their private space for remembering and reflecting upon death, Mr and Mrs Cutler would be able to gaze upon it, or touch it, daily as it became a focal means of remembering their son. The propeller grave marker originated from a crashed aeroplane and its placement in the grounds of their home as a form of 'spatialised memory making . . . emphasis[ing] the poignant nature of the death it marks' and 'through embodied engagement with such objects, and the spaces they inhabit, the presence of absence comes to be produced'.[70] In erecting the grave marker in their garden, Mr and Mrs Cutler could be deemed to be making a 'cultural strategy' to cope with their grief and sense of loss by sustaining some form of 'physical connection . . . to build a "living" social presence' for their son.[71]

The propeller grave marker is now displayed within a museum glass cabinet with other, unrelated, objects of conflict. It 'provides a succinct, yet powerful narrative of salvage – the object was threatened by the prospect of loss, but it was "found", retrieved and preserved in the museum'.[72] This leads to the suggestion that the object has 'agency', as since the grave marker was found in a garden 'it must have exercised some form of attraction at the point of initial discovery' and, indeed, Colonel Cartwright recognized its significance as the marker of a grave of a First World War aviator.[73] On its arrival at the museum, the grave marker was catalogued and placed in a glass cabinet alongside a card bearing a brief typed description, such 'an insertion into narrative that at once "makes sense" of its very presence in the Museum' and representing another event in its social life.[74]

Discussion

Adopting a biographical approach reveals how the meaning of a propeller grave marker changes over time as it becomes recycled and recontextualized, illustrating connections between people and things. Propeller grave markers became distinctive and highly visual repositories for an aviator's flying experiences, often told as stories which became his commemorative legacy as objects and their tales became entwined in social interactions. The erection of a grave marker likely influenced the thoughts and actions of others, mediating social agency, for encountering one could induce an emotional response. Once erected, the grave marker becomes an agent of communication and attraction, visually informing individuals and groups of a pilot's death. Such objects have the potential to communicate to people the way they should feel emotionally. Indeed, Bourdieu's concept of *habitus* established that objects help people learn how to act appropriately, thereby giving credence to the idea that objects make us as much as we make them as they become part of who we are.[75]

Spaces attract activities and, when the bereaved travelled to the Western Front to visit the graves of their lost loved ones, the social dimensions of such visits were materialized as an 'interaction between the living and the dead'. Visitors placed, and sometimes planted, flowers by the grave, they kissed the grave marker and traced their fingers along the inscribed name, or simply spoke the name of the dead aviator to themselves as they remembered him. Such 'embodied practices' allowed the visiting bereaved to 'create' and maintain 'memory links' with the dead, articulating the various spaces of their pilgrimage with specific levels of privately recalled memory.[76]

The re-placement of a propeller grave marker, from the Western Front to the Home Front, whether re-sited in a cemetery, inside a church, a churchyard, museum, or private grounds evokes a relationship between the living and the dead, providing a point of contact with the deceased that changes over time as 'the living and dead [are] provided with shared spaced through efforts of memory'.[77] Initially, the grave marker is 'infused with a bittersweet quality evoking that which they cannot replace and providing touchstones for inchoate feelings of grief'.[78] By placing the grave marker in a space of meaning, for example, the back garden of the family home where the aviator would have played as a child, provides a visual and material focus within the arena where the social lives of his parents and siblings are played out – in a sense he is reincorporated into the everyday world of the living. Here we see how a space becomes a place where the passage of time is fixed.

The social life of a propeller grave marker can be divided into seven periods, identified here as events or social interactions: (a) pre-acquisition event; (b) acquisition event; (c) manufacture event; (d) erection event and funeral; (e) post-war visitation event; (f) lost or destroyed event; and (g) donation elsewhere event. This biographical approach gave their stories new depth and dimension, new layers of meaning not only for the propeller grave marker but also the war in the air overall.

What happens before and after the erection of the grave marker – in terms of the pre-acquisition, acquisition, and manufacture events – is significant for its anthropological and archaeological interpretation. Materiality is a cultural process and: '[i]n a sense, looking at what happens before and after the artefact is more significant than the artefact itself; that is, the terms of materiality rather than material culture itself and the differential ability of individuals to participate in these processes is more important'.[79] By using aviators' diaries, letters, and books, it was possible for these 'mute objects to speak'.[80] The propeller grave markers were revealed as repositories for an aviator's conflict flying experiences. The story of both the aviator's death and how the propeller came to be acquired, for example, by 'souveniring' and the grave marker's subsequent manufacture that contributes to the overall value, meaning, and significance of the object as a commemorative legacy.

Chapter 9

Souvenirs and Trench Art: Making Sense of Wooden Things

As an example of wartime materiel, First World War aeroplanes possess value as anthropological-archaeological objects through their cultural associations and legacies. Here I offer an archaeological/anthropological study of aviation-related trench art, which examines the sensory and affective connections between crashed aircraft parts made from wood, metal, and linen through the study of archives, collections, and photographs. It presents new insights into First World War aviation by revealing how the dismantling of aeroplane components and the making of trench art retains a connection to the flight experience of First World War aviators as well as creating and maintaining new relationships between objects and people.

In documenting and analysing the First World War in the air, it is important to establish the fate of the remains of numerous crashed aeroplanes – especially wooden propellers (see Chapter 10 for linen coverings and metal engine struts). Case studies presented here deal with:

(a) objects taken from a crashed aeroplane and retained as a souvenir by an aviator or a squadron.[1] No. 56 Squadron, for example, was known to have a German wooden propeller fixed to a wall 'between two black canvas crosses cut from enemy aircraft, a three-ply board was fixed in a carved wooden frame. The number of the squadron was at the head: below were the names of the men who had won decorations';[2]

(b) pieces of wood from a crashed aeroplane that were reworked into trench art.

Pilots' experiences of the First World War were embodied in souvenirs and trench art whose social lives have endured for over a century. Such 'objects hold within themselves the worlds of their creators' and are 'endowed with the personal characteristics' of the aviators, thus transgressing the boundaries between objects and people.[3] The biographical approach used throughout this book highlights that things cannot be fully comprehended at just one point in their lives because they change throughout their existence.

Aviation-related Souvenirs: An Air War of 'Souveniring'

The First World War became known as 'the War of Souvenirs' because from 'the moment [they] landed in France [they] started collecting and giving away souvenirs'.[4] Most aviators wanted souvenirs from the war and many were sent home to their families, or retained by the aviator himself, many with a story attached concerning survival or acquisition. Gordon Taylor remembers shooting down a German Rumpler reconnaissance biplane, witnessing the observer jump to his death. He was given the tail-skid from the wreck as a souvenir, writing 'I had no wish for it; but to avoid explanations I took it, and afterwards gave it to Uncle Bottom'.[5]

Souveniring was a widespread craze. Even the Zeppelin raids against England led to civilians collecting items from the airship because a Zeppelin when 'properly dissected, provided quite a large number of souvenirs. Charming brooches and scarfpins can be made from the wire, and the framework will provide material for an almost unlimited number of articles of household utility'.[6] German airmen also participated in souveniring as Manfred von Richthofen's study is known to have been decorated with trophies or souvenirs from his victories including even a British aeroplane engine as the chandelier. In addition, aeroplane identification numbers were cut off the surfaces of Allied aeroplanes and used to decorate his study walls.[7]

However, not everybody wished for souvenirs for Maurice Baring wrote:

> I went to Ypres . . . and had a real leisurely exploration of the place. I spent some time in the ruined cathedral. The organ was still intact, but the staircase leading up to it was destroyed. . . . In the sacristy of the cathedral there were a lot of books and missals quite intact. A harvest of souvenirs for those who wanted such things. I had no inclination to take even a chip of brick away.[8]

Several photographs (for example, Figure 22) depict a crashed German aeroplane being looted by souvenir hunters and it is evident that, whilst the linen insignia on the starboard side of the aeroplane has already been removed, the propeller is still intact, but for how much longer?

Causing a German pilot to crash-land on British lines, the British fighter ace James McCudden VC described flying after a damaged German aeroplane and following it down as it crashed. He landed alongside it as he wished to ensure the German pilot did not escape. He left his engine idling away whilst he went to look at the German and found 'two groups of Australian infantry . . . Everything of any value in the way of souvenirs on the machine had already gone, for although I landed a very short time after the Hun came down, the Tommies had already taken what was worth taking.'[9]

Figure 22. *A shot-down German Fokker biplane, Cambrai front, France. The aeroplane tail and fuselage have been stripped of the painted cloth insignia by troops as souvenirs.* (Author's collection)

Arthur Gould Lee remembered waiting for a tender from his squadron to salvage the damaged Sopwith Camel he had been flying and, whilst walking, he passed the wreckage of a German aeroplane that had been shot down. He noted that 'souvenir hunters had removed everything detachable, including the cockpit instruments, the machine guns, and the fabric Iron Crosses'.[10] Other aeroplane crashes completely wrecked the aeroplane but there were still pieces attractive to souvenir hunters, the wreckage providing completely different reifications of the flying experience for non-flyers.

The Imperial War Museum in London has a wooden propeller from a shot-down German Gotha bomber aeroplane. The story which contextualizes it belongs to Lieutenant Anthony John Arkell of No. 39 Squadron (Home Defence) who piloted a Bristol Fighter. The propeller bears a small brass plate commemoratively engraved thus:

>DEVIL IN THE DUSK
>EAST HAM
>May 19/20, 1918

The brass plate marks historical geographical time and space. On the night of 19 May 1918, Lieutenant Anthony Arkell and his observer, Private A.T.C. Stagg, flew a night patrol in Arkell's aeroplane, Bristol Fighter C4636, that he had named 'Devil in the Dusk'. They sighted a German Gotha bomber flying at 10,000ft. Arkell opened fire at a range of 200yd. The enemy aeroplane fired continuously at Devil in the Dusk but Arkell managed to skilfully manoeuvre in such a way as to allow his observer to find a target that offered the best possible advantage for attack. Private Stagg was able to open heavy fire upon the German aeroplane at close range. The Gotha was engulfed in flames and subsequently crashed to the ground. Lieutenant Arkell was awarded the Military Cross for conspicuous gallantry, whilst Private Stagg was awarded the Military Medal for displaying great courage and skill.[11] The disparity in medals highlights the perceived differences in both rank and class as if one's social class was matched by a different ability to sense/suffer danger and pain.

The next morning, Lieutenant Arkell went to the crash site to view the remains of the crashed Gotha (see Figure 16). After viewing the remains, Arkell wrote about the crash in a letter to his father, informing that he 'brought back a small bit of canvas, a bit of charred wood, and one German cartridge case as small souvenirs, but it will be topping if I can get that propeller. I also got a three-ply box that contained the belt of ammunition for the Hun machine gun, slightly charred'.[12] The wrecked aeroplane, now a pile of scrap, and the dead pilot become interchangeable through a process of objectification providing a means of comprehending the relationship between subjects and objects as new endeavours, such as souveniring, become possible. Clearly these souvenirs and the story attached to them would provide a talking point for all who saw them for years to come.

Trench Art

James McCudden VC, writing about a crashed German aeroplane, reported, 'flying back to my aerodrome with my machine laden with various interesting fittings from the Hun machine . . . To this day I have a very nice cigarette box made out of the propeller of that Hun'.[13] This is an example of trench art made from war materiel. Whilst McCudden claimed a propeller made souvenir cigarette box, others had propellers recycled into trinket boxes, photograph frames, clocks, and walking sticks. All such objects had a practical use and were reminders of their owners' pre-war lives.

Trench art can be regarded as the materialization of airmen's relationships and experiences of being in the First World War and, as such, provides significant and valuable insight into how individual aviators coped with their unique experiences of war. During the inter war years, examples of trench art 'could be seen in half the houses in Britain' as they became representative of meaningful First World War events and experiences.[14]

In *Auntie Mabel's War*, Marian Wenzel and John Cornish's account of Mabel Jeffrey, a nurse who served on the Western Front and in the Balkans during the First World War, Mabel's niece, Mrs Turner, reminisces about a trench-art vase her aunt bought back from the war, commenting:

> Yes, that thing by the fireplace with the flowers on it is really a shell case . . . from the First World War. [Aunt Mabel] brought [it] back for her parents; I thought it was an awfully morbid thing . . . I could have thought of nicer things to bring back . . . It got to Granny's house and then it came here . . . I'd have put it under the hydrangeas. I often look at it and wonder how many men its shell killed.[15]

Walking Sticks from Flying Machines
Duncan Grinnell-Milne remembered 'on the way to the barge I passed M.C. He was whistling and slashing the heads off thistles with a cane made from the propeller of the German aeroplane he had brought down'.[16] Similarly, McCudden, writing about a French Morane Saulnier biplane that was badly shot-up, recorded 'the propeller had four bullet holes in it, and at this present time I still have a walking stick made from the remains of that propeller'.[17]

In terms of acquiring raw materials and making items, it was common for airmen to claim pieces of crashed aeroplane as souvenirs of the event and then have someone, often the squadron armourer, recraft the souvenirs into trench art that would be useful and/or a memento of the crash. London's Imperial War Museum has a walking stick crafted from the wooden propeller of the First World War aeroplane flown by Lieutenant Leonard Stockton Smith that was shot down at Messines Ridge on 7 June 1917.[18] The handle has a hallmarked silver shield-shaped plaque fixed to the top baring an engraved inscription: 'Lt. Stockton Smith from 1 Squadron Royal Flying Corps. Made from the propeller of a machine brought down on Messines Ridge – June 7th 1917'. It is imbued with Stockton Smith's sentient experiences whilst flying during the Battle of Messines Ridge. Like most servicemen, he did not leave a diary of, or write a book about, his wartime experiences, but the writings of other pilots give us an idea of what he might have seen, heard, smelt, and felt when his aeroplane crashed.

The assault on Messines Ridge, a German stronghold, was preceded by the simultaneous detonation of large mines tunnelled beneath the ridge. On 7 June 1917, fighter pilot Captain William Bond was patrolling the front line hunting for enemy reconnaissance aeroplanes spying on the British artillery positions for the German gunners. Bond was flying at 12,000ft and he gives an account which is representative of what Lieutenant Stockton Smith may have witnessed:

a patch of country about 20 miles long and 12 miles deep was . . . ablaze . . . the fields and woods and roads were livid with the flashes of our guns . . . Towards the eastern edge of the smoky belt was a constant band of white shrapnel bursts, like snowdrops overcrowded in a garden border, and before them and behind them and on both sides of them the continuous eruptions of red earth and dust where the increasing rain of high explosive shells was [sic] falling.[19]

Bond had a narrow escape one morning when, leading his first patrol, he was hit by a salvo of Archie.[20] He described the experience to his wife, Aimée, to whom he wrote a daily letter, as she did him:

I felt a violent shock on the joy stick. The whole machine shuddered . . . The right aileron control had been shot away! I kept my nose down, heading for home, and found that I could still get a sufficient amount of wing controls to make slow turns. Landing became a problem, as the moment I switched off the engine the right wing dropped. I flew right onto the ground, though, without smashing anything.

I have the broken parts of the rod and the armourer is going to produce some souvenir from it for you.[21]

It is possible to see how the birth of a souvenir infused with individual meaning might come into being as Captain Bond retrieved broken pieces of his crashed aeroplane as a souvenir. He then engaged the squadron armourer to make the pieces into a walking stick, which represented the day he survived an aeroplane crash. Although pivotal to the acquisition event, Bond could not, however, claim a tactile relationship with the object borne of working the material himself.

William Bond was killed in action, flying his Nieuport Scout B1688, on 22 July 1917, at Sallaumines, France.[22] Pilot William MacLanachan (writing under the pseudonym 'McScotch') remembered packing Bond's belongings, 'the shaving brush with the morning's soap still wet on it; all to make room for another pilot who might share the same fate within a week or a month'.[23] William Bond does not have a grave but his name is inscribed upon the Arras Flying Services Memorial.[24] With no grave to visit, Aimée continued to write letters to her husband after his death. After attending an evening performance of a revue, she wrote to her dead husband:

The lights in the auditorium were low, and from then onwards, in that crowded smoky place, I saw you vividly. Never since the news came have I seen you so vividly.

Your stick, the one made from the broken propeller, with the band of the fragment of aileron control, was in my hand. It goes everywhere with me.[25]

The stick became an emotional focus in the home of the bereaved. Touching it, as she did every day, heightened Aimée's sense of loss. The walking stick became a poignant memento for her, and, perhaps, a substitute for her dead husband. It is not known what became of the stick. At some later point, perhaps following Aimée's death, the stick may have become an anonymous object as future generations may not have known the story behind it. The immediacy of its emotional significance and value would have weakened and perhaps been forever lost.

The end of the First World War gave rise to examples of cultural influence as new books, magazines, and films came into being. Following the war, Captain William Bond's wife, Aimée McHardy, published *An Airman's Wife*, possibly an attempt to cope with the loss of her husband and to keep his memory alive. The book itself is material culture and owed its creation to the First World War. The publication of the letters that William Bond wrote to his wife, many of them love letters, have a powerful effect on people's emotions even today.

Landscape Painting on a Broken Propeller
The colourful scene reproduced in Plate 15 was painted by Corporal J. Willey on a section of a Sopwith Camel's wooden propeller.[26] Willey was an artist in his spare time and specialized in painting RFC aircraft shooting down Germans over the Ypres landscape, 'with kite balloons floating over shell-broken trees, clouds and shell-bursts in the sky'.[27] The scene depicts a German *Drachen* observation balloon falling through the sky in flames with a RFC Morane Saulnier flying through anti-aircraft explosions.[28] Willey's paintings represent human activity that captured a moment of aerial conflict. In painting what he himself had witnessed, Willey offers us further experiences as his multi-sensorial past mingles with our visual present so that we might understand and know *his* past. Willey gifted this painted propeller to Sergeant C.M. Smith, 676th Field Ambulance, Royal Army Medical Corps.

In *Into the Blue*, Captain Norman Macmillan remembered his Brigade padre's servant, Corporal Willey. Willey painted a similar image on another broken propeller from one of Macmillan's own Sopwith Camels.[29] Macmillan's painted cut-down propeller blade might have served as a reminder of his flying experiences. After serving in France with the Highland Light Infantry for sixteen months, he joined the RFC in 1916, and in 1917 joined No. 45 Squadron where he flew a Sopwith Strutter biplane.[30] When his squadron was re-equipped with Sopwith Camels he gained his unit's first Camel victory on 25 August 1917.

Macmillan related one episode whilst flying in the Second Battle of Passchendaele (26 October–10 November 1917) which was the culminating attack during the Third Battle of Ypres. He recalled flying on reconnaissance to report enemy movements during a heavy rainstorm on 26 October 1917. These observations had to be reported promptly by writing on a card which was then placed in a weighted canvas bag with red and yellow streamer tails and subsequently dropped over the designated report centre. Macmillan recalled how difficult it was to write whilst flying a Camel at low height in rough weather. The aeroplane was unstable. He could feel the heaviness of the tail. It was essential that he remained continually alert in order that he could adjust the controls to match the flying conditions whilst simultaneously looking out for other aircraft flying in the vicinity and being forever ready to dodge machine-gun fire from the ground.[31]

The skill involved in flying an aeroplane relies on the relationship between vision and touch, for example, through hand-eye coordination, for the pilot must, at all times, maintain a look out whilst simultaneously keeping an eye on the horizon to hold the aeroplane on an even keel. Indeed, when I was flying a Tiger Moth the pilot instructed me:

> See how the nose is too high above the horizon? You've got to lower the nose. Ease the column to the right, because we need to go right to miss the rain. Ease it to the right. A bit more. . . . Right, column to the left . . . that's good.

A hook has been fitted to the upper edge of Willey's propeller painting indicating that, at one point, it was hung on somebody's wall as a memento of the war and perhaps also a visual reminder and a talking point for all who saw it. The propeller painting was eventually donated to the Imperial War Museum and is now stored in its archives; for the moment it can be regarded as having suffered a 'social death' – though it could be construed that my research has added a further biographical footnote.[32]

Propeller Photograph Frame
It was common to frame photographs in trench-art photograph frames (see Plate 16) such as this one I purchased from a Belgian dealer of First World War memorabilia. Some of the trench-art propeller tip photograph frames were plain, like this one, whereas others were works of art, often bearing intricate carvings as well.

John McGavock Grider wrote, 'we decided that since our lives were in jeopardy we ought to have our pictures taken to preserve our likeness for posterity'.[33] Such a photograph has the ability to create a memory of a moment in time. The photograph of the young man wearing the uniform of a British soldier in the photograph frame in Plate 16 was printed on a postcard and the photograph was taken by the London Portrait Company, 160 Victoria Road, Aldershot. Perhaps he too had his photograph taken for his family and friends before departing to fight in the war. The photograph at the bottom of the frame depicts a group gathering which could be the soldier's friends and/or family. On the reverse of the postcard-style photograph is a hand-written message:

> Mrs Deverall, New Ferry.
>
> Dear Dave,
> Am sending this just to let you at least see the group which had such a pleasant time at Barry. This was taken at Cardiff when returning home. We are all supposed to be smiling.
>   The real purpose of writing is to give you Mrs Deverall's address – do drop her a line straight away, Dave, she will think so much of it. Love to all.
>   In haste, Tom

'Tom' may well be the gentleman seated in the middle of the front row of the group photograph and has given the address of the contact as being in New Ferry which is a town in the Wirral area of northwest England. My interpretation of this object is that the photograph shows a group of friends, or a mix of family and friends, including Tom. It is possible that they were not all known to each other, only to Tom, who thereby connected them all. It seems that they all had an enjoyable and memorable trip to Barry and returned home via Cardiff. Before Tom left for war he arranged for this photograph to be taken.

Tom may have had the photograph mounted in the trench-art-style photograph frame, perhaps imparting the message to friends and family not to worry about him and that if he did not return then they were to remember the happy times they had together in Barry. He may have purchased the propeller photograph frame as a souvenir or he may have been given it by a friend or a relative, who may, perhaps, have been in the RFC. He need not have obtained it directly from a member of the RFC for such items were readily available on the Home Front as well as the Western Front. Propellers, for example, also had to be replaced if they were riddled with bullets. Indeed, when new pilot Duncan Grinnell-Milne returned from an operational flight during which contact was made with the enemy, he remembers being asked by the Flight Commander, 'how the devil did you manage to get two bullets through that propeller of yours?' and then went on '[t]hose shots came from your own gun! You'll have to get a new propeller, and these things cost money. . . . How would you like it if the Government said you had to fork out forty pounds?'[34]

The photograph frame has two nails linked by a length of shoelace-type material on the back to enable it to hang from a wall to become the subject of someone's gaze. The wooden frame is covered in dents and scratches and has a couple of deep cracks in places, held together by a glue-like substance, the glue perhaps working hard to keep the memories alive. This almost personifies the glue and suggests it is acting through a sense of purpose.

Once the propeller had been acquired, it may have been made into trench art at someone's request, that is made to order, or it may have been made on spec, and perhaps sold on for profit. Is there perhaps a connection between the soldier in the photograph and the RFC? Many soldiers transferred from the trenches to the RFC. Perhaps Tom wished to join the RFC or maybe he had a brother or a friend in the RFC? We will never know. After the war, it was made to hold two photographs. It is also ornamental and may have been on display in someone's home as an object of loss for the bereaved as emotions were worked out as families tried to come to terms with the tragedy of war. The photograph frame is now the object of academic research and resides in my study where it has been the subject of tactile engagement as I explored and documented it. It has been measured, polished, photographed, and dismantled to retrieve the photographs to discover if anything was written on their reverse sides in an attempt to reveal clues that would help in retrieving its story. It is one example amongst many such items where an object's life story can be carefully unwound albeit incompletely and somewhat speculatively.

Propeller Dinner Gong
Dinner gongs were popular in Edwardian Britain and beyond 1910 when George V ruled. Announcing mealtimes in the homes of the wealthy, the sound regulated people's lives as well as coinciding with the smell of dinner cooking. Trench-art dinner gongs were popular, being made from, for example, the wooden propeller and engine parts of an aeroplane, as well as empty shell cases, and continued to be used after the war. This is an ironic statement when one considers the reality of another type of gong used on the Western Front for, in an attempt to break the stalemate of trench warfare, chemical warfare in the form of gas attacks was introduced. Indeed:

> The little golden gongs, like the bells of a Burmese temple, would recall men from idle tasks to the disciplines, more binding than those of religion, and in an ecstasy of terror they would thrust their heads into the masks which might save their souls 'S.O.S.!' Up went the signal in rocket flares; and the cry 'Gas!' echoes along the line. In British, French and German trenches, this ritual was observed.[35]

As dinner can be smelt, so too can gas, both instances of olfactory warnings – 'the odour of gas is often likened to the smell of familiar tangible "things" on the home front. Chlorine smells like bleach; phosgene recalls freshly mown hay'.[36]

As soldiers responded to the sound of a gong warning of incoming gas and the urgent necessity to don their gas masks, many families experienced the sound of the dinner gong made from war materiel calling them to dinner. This highlights the contradictions of warfare in terms of the crashed aeroplane from which the propeller came from, the ironies of association in terms of the smell of gas during the First World War competing with the smell of dinner in times of peace. The propeller dinner gong is a poignant memory object whose meaning has been reconfigured from being an object of conflict to one imbued with memories of family dinners.

Propeller Clocks
Whilst many trench-art objects were made during the war, the majority of them were made after the Armistice of 11 November 1918, and many of these were commercially produced in the period 1918 to circa 1939.[37] Some of these objects were fashioned from war materiel sent home as mementoes and souvenirs of conflict by the returning aviators. They represented 'not the lived experience of its maker but the "secondhand" experience of its possessor/owner'.[38] Other souvenirs and mementoes could be linked to airmen's personal experiences and would therefore have a story attached to them.[39]

There is evidently a commercial element to some post-war trench art as companies advertised their services to personalize such mementoes and this often involved mounting them on decorative bases, perhaps recycling them into a clock or a dinner gong or an ink stand. Such companies also managed to have a stock of ready-made or ready-to-be-made items from war materiel. Such instances are termed 'Mounted War Trophies'.[40]

In 1916, following a strafe, pilot Vernon Castle described in a letter to his wife how, the noise of a gun he fired caused a constant ringing in his ears.[41] Interestingly he mentioned that he had retained a shell case to take home with the intention of having:

> . . . it made into a lamp or something for Mother. Of course I'll have a lot of souvenirs for our home. *They will be interesting after the war.* I've got several now, so we can give some away. . . . I guess one will be able to buy them after the war, *but they won't be so interesting.* Mine will have a sort of little history attached . . .[42]

Such letters from pilots to their wives reveal how easy it was for souvenirs from the war to enter peoples' homes. Souvenirs of war had become a way of life and, if they had not already been made into a souvenir, plans would be underway to craft them into one after the war. During the conflict, it was acknowledged that it is preferable to have souvenirs with some sort of authentic story attached to them for, as Captain Castle's letter suggests, an object would be authentic if it had a story attached to it in which case one could ask the question, is an object 'real' if associated with the sender but 'fictionalized' if just purchased somewhere?

Many commercially made trench-art clocks were mounted on the wooden boss that formed the centre of a propeller blade (see Plate 17). They have no stories attached and are seemingly kept by museums as examples. Such propeller clocks were produced in the thousands and varied in quality from the plain to the extravagantly carved and it became fashionable to display them in the home. Visitors may have assumed that they were connected to personal war experiences when, in fact, they represented only a general reminder of the war. This clock is made of mahogany so would require the application of some sort of wax polish to prevent it from drying out. Such tactile activity would release smells into the domestic atmosphere, the act of polishing representing a silent and emotional temporal communication linking the present with the past. Certainly such clocks would have introduced punctuality and order into the home in terms of eating at a certain time, leaving for work at a certain time, going to bed at a certain time. It would also have introduced duties of tactility into the home in terms of having to use a key to wind the clock to keep time and to manually move the second hand to correct time.

Finally, a clock representing the First World War could also be a reminder of the concept of British Summer Time which was first adopted in Britain in 1916, during the First World War, when it was known as daylight saving time for the aim of its introduction was to facilitate better use of lighter hours. It was introduced to help the wartime economy; clocks sprung forward one hour during the spring and back one hour during the autumn, as they do today.

Pieces of crashed aeroplane were turned into trench art some of which found a resting place as memory objects in focal positions in the domestic household. These objects, and those described in the following chapter, created a new sensorial world for the bereaved as the emotional atmosphere within the household altered. Such tactile contact with the trench art as it is dusted and polished triggered memories of times gone by.

Chapter 10

Memories of Linen and Metal: Souvenirs and Trench Art

Linen

Linen was the skin of First World War aeroplanes, and was often removed from crashed aeroplanes as souvenirs (see Figure 15).[1] Although not obvious, this is an example of trench art – RFC personnel painted the insignia onto the linen of aeroplanes that were 'associated . . . with armed conflict'.[2]

Women were employed to sew linen onto aircraft wings and then paint them with dope, a poisonous substance made from nitro-cellulose. When the dope dried, the canvas shrunk, thus strengthening the wings. However, the women undertaking this task suffered from giddiness and headaches from breathing in the noxious fumes emitted by the dope. To counteract this, women employed in such tasks at the Bristol Tramways Shed in Brislington, whilst employed by the British and Colonial Aeroplane Company Limited, were given milk to drink, although there is no evidence of this being a successful antidote.[3] Hence aeroplane wings already caused human suffering before they reached the theatre of war. It is a tragic irony that some of the mothers, sisters, and wives employed in doping the linen may have lost their husbands, sons, and brothers who flew the aeroplanes made from the linen they had sewn and to which they had applied noxious dope.

On visiting the Shuttleworth Collection I walked through the workshop and experienced feelings of nausea due to the overpowering smell of dope, exhaust fumes, and oil. The smell evoked a bygone era. Museum staff had thoughtfully left out samples of linen that they were using to overhaul aeroplanes in the collection thereby allowing visitors an opportunity for tangible contact. It was paper thin and felt stiff and rough against the fingertips.

During the war it was common for pilots to personalize their aircraft by painting emblems and insignia upon the aircraft linen as a means of distinguishing them from the aeroplanes of other squadrons. Such individual markings did not meet with RFC approval, although they served a variety of purposes, such as boosting morale, striking fear into the opposing German aviators, and identifying individual pilots in the sky.⁴ In the early war years, the RFC was regarded as the cavalry of the air and, when war broke out, men who had been in the cavalry were deemed suitable to train as pilots.⁵ It is not known where the idea of painting insignia on aeroplanes originated but perhaps it had something to do with British knight heraldry as knights designed and displayed armorial bearings so that they might be identified in battle.⁶

Sometimes events conspire to give unique insights into the behaviours of war. Below are several examples of pilots who had insignia painted onto the linen of their aeroplanes that subsequently crashed and the linen insignia removed as souvenirs.

Schweinhund

Duncan Grinnell-Milne painted the words *Schweinhund* (because he had been called it so many times) in large white letters, on to the three-ply panel below the engine, on his bright-red SE5a aeroplane, No. C1149, mainly to annoy the enemy.⁷ He had even been tempted to sketch 'a portrait of the Kaiser on the radiator, painted so that when the shutters were opened and closed rapidly the Imperial moustaches would wiggle and the eyes blink – the idea being that a picture of the All Highest might put enemy machine-gunners off their aim'.⁸ His aeroplane survived the war and he cut from the side of *Schweinhund III* the linen panel upon which the name was painted and took it home with him as 'a vain reminder of the days of her greatness'.⁹

Black-faced Devil with Red Horns Insignia

The crew of Handley Page O/100 1466 painted a snarling, black-faced devil embellished with red horns, red eyebrows, and red eyes on a mud-brown background onto the linen of the aeroplane. The devil's mouth is wide open, the whole open-mouth cavity is red as though entry into it would lead to a burning hell. This may have been a warning to the enemy as well as an act of bravado on the part of the young Handley Page crew to enemy aircraft who could outmanoeuvre them. To the bottom right of the devil's face a total of fourteen images of bombs, displayed in three rows, have been painted in orange – these may have been mission tallies and, therefore, the sign of an experienced pilot. The greyish-white painted serial number 1466 has been cut from the aeroplane's tail fabric and has been attached to the left side of the painting of the devil. The painted linen has been placed in a glass-fronted wooden frame to become a memory object, reifying the experiences of the crew who flew her and representative of the acquisition and manufacturing events of its social life.

Author Rob Langham describes the events of the night of 22 August 1918 when Handley Page O/100 1466 was destroyed on returning from bombing Frankfurt. Following a forced landing at Autreville, France, early that morning, due to double engine failure, 1466 caught fire and was destroyed; only the tail survived. The engines failed because anti-aircraft fire had pierced a petrol tank causing the petrol-soaked starboard wing to catch fire. On escaping the crashed aeroplane, the crew crouched to the ground to avoid the exploding ammunition caused by the heat of the fire.[10] It was as though they themselves were escaping from the unbearable heat of hell advertised by their devil's insignia.

I would suggest that the noise prompted an overwhelming sensorial bodily experience in terms of hearing and feeling the ammunition explode, feeling the warmth of the heat and feeling the flow of adrenaline course through the body, together with the overwhelming sense of sheer relief afforded by their escape. The serial number, 1466, was cut from the fabric of the tail probably as a souvenir. The insignia was acquired by Squadron Commander Horace Buss of No. 216 Squadron (who had previously piloted 1466). It is not clear how he acquired it but he later gave it to Wing Commander Browne in 1930. Wing Commander Browne's logbook reveals that he flew this last flight on 1466.[11]

In 2013, the devil insignia featured in an exhibition of aircraft nose art at the RAF Museum Cosford and is now on permanent display at the RAF Museum London thus adding a further event to its social life and attracting the gaze of all who visit.

Love-heart Insignia
Canadian pilot Major William Barker flew in France and Italy during the years 1917–1918. He flew Sopwith Camel B6313 with a love-heart motif painted on the linen tail. It was his personal insignia and representative of a reaction to an event in his life that he did not approve of. Major Barker customized B6313 and it was redecorated to his individual preference on at least three occasions. Flying first in France, Barker was then posted to the Italian Front.[12] In terms of successful 'kills', Barker did not have any in other Sopwith Camels, and no pilot other than Barker had successful kills in B6313.[13] On his move to the Italian Front to lead No. 139 Squadron, he was, unusually, allowed to retain B6313.[14] He had a red heart with an arrow through painted on to the vertical fin of his aeroplane (see Figure 23).

Two months later, the painted heart symbol was reversed, because, allegedly, Barker was so upset about his new assignment in Italy that he felt as if he had been stabbed through the heart. In a fit of pique he instructed someone to paint the arrow-in-heart on the tail, and informed any pilot who inquired that it was his own bleeding heart. He made sure that his thirty-eight victories in B6313 were marked on the left front wing strut.[15] This was to advertise his success as a pilot and may also have been a means of unnerving the enemy who would know that they were facing a highly experienced pilot.

David Roberts' letter in *Windsock International* imparts additional information useful to enthusiasts wishing to make an accurate miniature model of B6313.[16]

Figure 23. *Major William Barker standing in front of Sopwith Camel B6313. The white painted arrow is visible on the port side of the vertical fin.* (Courtesy of Cross & Cockade International)

Whilst working at the RAF Museum London, he remembered Barker's former engine fitter attending the museum to donate the fin fabric. The fitter recalled that this and some other RAF aeroplanes had had their upper and side surfaces repainted in an unspecified Italian paint following a major overhaul, which included some recovering of linen. Roberts took a Methuen sample, but it got lost during one of his many relocations.[17] He recalled that the green was quite bright, like the colour of pea soup. Unfortunately, framing for display purposes had hidden the traces of green around the edges, leaving only black visible. The heart motif was painted a dark blood-red, applied over an earlier version in RAF roundel red, still visible in places. Thus, he is imparting information that would allow model makers to accurately reproduce the colour scheme of Barker's aeroplane. The engine fitter recalled that the day Barker left, he removed the fin fabric with a knife and handed one side each to his mechanics, saying 'Little Souvenir, fellas. Thanks for everything'.[18]

The tail fin is infused with Barker's wartime flying experiences. He was, for example, awarded the Victoria Cross 'in recognition of bravery of the highest possible order'.[19] On the morning of 27 October 1918, he attacked an enemy aeroplane, witnessing it break up in the air. He was severely wounded in both legs and his left arm was shattered. He willed himself to remain awake and alert in order to maintain control of the aeroplane but he fell in and out of consciousness, almost losing the struggle. Despite this, he managed to fight off formations of German Fokker aeroplanes, destroying four of them. He successfully returned to his base where he crash-landed.[20]

The effects of Barker's injuries remained with him throughout the rest of his life in the forms of visual scars and recurring felt pain – the painted tail fin is therefore imbued with bodily memory. On viewing the scars in later life he might have felt the aching of the repaired broken bones, reminding him of his wartime experiences.

Barker first flew B6313 on 30 September 1917 and for the last time on 29 September 1918, by which time he had accounted for 379 hours and 25 minutes of the aircraft's total flying time of 404 hours and 10 minutes. B6313 was dismantled on 2 October 1918, and Barker attempted to retain its clock as a souvenir.[21] But he was asked to return it the next day. Indeed, pilot Arthur Gould Lee experienced a similar problem when his aeroplane's 'watch' was misappropriated by a souvenir hunter. He concedes that the watches are 'very nice' and that many pilots would like to own one. He explains how you are meant to remove it from the aeroplane when you are forced to land but on this occasion he simply forgot and:

> Everyone thinks I swiped [it] myself [and now] there's a howl from the equipment people, and I'm having to fill [in] forms swearing I haven't stolen it, and don't know who did. Strange they don't mind you losing an aeroplane, but a watch, . . . that's different![22]

The love-heart insignia was displayed at RAF Museum Cosford as part of an aircraft art exhibition from December 2012 to June 2013.[23] It was then on display at the RAF Museum London, thus adding another chapter to its 'social life' and affording the viewing public a sense of the past as they wonder why Barker had his heart broken.

Aircraft Linen as Paul Klee's Canvas
The Germans also recycled linen from crashed aeroplanes during the First World War. The Swiss-German artist Paul Klee served in the German Army and was assigned to the Workshop Company where 'we presented ourselves not simply as painters, but as artistic painters'. The Company clerk told them, 'we were going to get work . . . that would enable us to put our art to the test' – they were given the job of varnishing aeroplane wings.[24] Consequently many of these aircraft ended up resembling Klee's fine art pieces.[25] He was then transferred to Flying School 5 as head painter in the Construction Squad to paint lozenge patterns on repaired aircraft, such camouflage aimed at making the visible invisible.[26]

In an interview with Sabine Rewald at the New York Metropolitan Museum of Art, Paul Klee's son, Felix Klee, remembered that his father painted on aeroplane linen which he had retrieved from a crashed aeroplane, cutting off pieces of linen with scissors. He did this whilst he was stationed at the Flying School in Gersthofen where he was assigned in January 1917 to do a desk job in the paymaster's office of the Royal Bavarian Flying School.[27] The painting is entitled *Libido of the Forest* and is now stored at the Metropolitan Museum of Art, New York, as part of the Berggruen Klee Collection.

Paul Klee witnessed several aeroplane crashes, writing:

> This week we had three fatal casualties; one man was smashed by the propeller, the other two crashed from the air! Yesterday a fourth man came ploughing with a loud bang into the roof of the workshop. Had been flying too low, caught on a telegraph pole, bounced on the roof of the factory, turned a somersault, and collapsed upside down in a heap of wreckage.[28]

Such events may have influenced Paul Klee to paint *Falling and Gliding Bird* in 1919, which 'depicts a large bird come [*sic*] hurtling down within seconds of a fatal crash in a desolate landscape'.[29]

The scavenged linen, as an example of trench art, represents an object used in warfare that is recycled during the war and recirculated in peaceful times by being exhibited in a museum. Klee may have regarded the aeroplane linen as simply a discarded object. When gazing at the painting today, visitors likely will not know that the linen came from an aeroplane crash of the First World War. Klee was not alone in transforming war materiel into trench art for fellow German artist Kurt Schwitters did so and described his creations as 'a campaign to combat chaos by salvaging the broken pieces left after the Great War'.[30] The linen and the painting are infused with Klee's wartime experiences and the attendance of viewing visitors to the museum highlights unusual legacies and associations beyond the conflict that gave birth to the object.

Metal

Trench Art Models of Miniature Biplanes

Second Lieutenant Frank Wayman Ely enlisted in the Royal Engineers in April 1915, aged 17½ years. After training, in 1916, he was posted to France on active service for sixteen months. During this time, he made two ornamental trench-art aeroplanes, now exhibited at the Shuttleworth Collection (see Plates 18 and 19).[31] These were popular items, and tended to be made whilst on active service.

The museum has captured the individuality of Lieutenant Ely in its display of his models and, importantly includes details of how the models were made – information not often available as servicemen rarely described them. These models embody the passing of time which began when Lieutenant Ely created his tool kit. Evidently, he did not have a screwdriver because he used a broken penknife to do that job. He also fabricated a home-made vice. Then followed the 'acquisition event' as he obtained the necessary war materiel to make the models. Some of the brass parts originated from the ruined organ in Arras Cathedral after the building had been shelled, perhaps an incidence of Ely indulging in 'souveniring'. Ely spent many hours laboriously making up the brass parts that were to be component parts of the models. The two models represent 'semantically dense item[s] that embodied periods and places scattered across the battle-zone landscape'.[32]

In 1917, Lieutenant Ely returned to England to attend a flying school where he successfully trained and was commissioned as a Second Lieutenant in November 1917. He resumed active service in France in 1918, joining No. 20 Squadron, but, after only fourteen days of flying he was killed when his Bristol F.2B aeroplane was shot down in flames near Brancourt on 8 October 1918 – just 28 days before the Armistice was signed.[33] Lieutenant Ely has no known grave and his name is inscribed on the Arras Flying Services Memorial at Faubourg-d'Amiens Cemetery, in Arras. This is a memorial to the missing commemorating almost a thousand airmen from the RFC, RNAS, and RAF who were killed on the Western Front from spring 1916 to August 1918 and who have no known grave.

Ely's trench art was probably not made in the trenches but away from enemy lines, perhaps on local leave. His trench art reveals how he spent some of his spare time and how he coped with his experiences of being a soldier in the First World War. The fact that he made models of biplanes may be an indication of his interest in, or intent on, becoming a pilot in the RFC, an aim he clearly achieved. He may have given the model aeroplanes to his family before he died, or they may have been returned to the family upon his death, and subsequently transformed into household ornaments.

As we have now seen many times, a biographical approach to objects facilitates the identification of the 'acquisition' and 'manufacturing events' in the 'social life' of the material investigated here. In particular, the model biplanes crafted by Lieutenant Ely from war materiel, some of which he had personally 'souvenired', embody and reify the circumstances of acquisition. This makes apparent how 'new meanings saturated matter in the initial stages of the production' and the crafted model biplanes become 'attached to the individual through a range of memory making events'.[34] Such attachments could be seen as authenticating the object in terms of wartime experience.

The biplane models reveal Lieutenant Ely's individuality and creativity, and as war materiel was 'transformed, symbolically and physically', the resulting trench-art items becoming 'a hybrid that represented [an aviator's] individuality – a meshing of personality, physical skill, wartime experience, and available raw material'.³⁵ Ely did not survive the war and the model biplanes he made became his memorial. Now on display at the Shuttleworth Collection within the confined space of a glass cabinet, these objects are 'three-dimensional biograph[ies] of war experience' and a legacy of conflict.³⁶

Letter Openers and Button Hooks
Letter openers (see Plate 20) and button hooks (see Plate 21) are two examples of functional trench art. Machine tools would have been necessary to make button hooks so it is probable that they were made in repair shops behind the lines during the war, although they continued to be made several years after the war.³⁷ This demonstrates that it is not always easy to categorize such items.

Both these items have RFC metal buttons attached to the ends (see Plate 22). The acquisition and manufacturing events of this trench art can be connected to members of the Chinese Labour Corps, whose members scavenged for war materiel which they used to make souvenir trench-art items for soldiers and aviators from used bullets, grenades, and shell cases.³⁸ Evidently skilled in the appropriation of the buttons of regiments or squadrons stationed in their vicinity, they used these to personalize trench-art objects which they then sold as souvenirs to the servicemen and aviators of these very same regiments and squadrons.

The Chinese Labour Corps continued to make such souvenirs after the war because their battlefield clearance and body retrieval duties gave them ready access to war materiel. It was also the case that the trench-art objects which they made were especially favoured souvenirs for battlefield visitors, likely because of their more exotic designs – dragons and Chinese figures and inscriptions.

Button hooks were not issued to aviators as official items of equipment though they may have been used by a batman dressing a pilot officer and a large number of trench-art button hooks were made.³⁹

Conclusions

Whilst the industrial warfare of the First World War, a war of materiel, caused unprecedented death and destruction, Chapters 9 and 10 reveal that it also instigated creativity and individuality in unexpected ways and that sometimes became the commemorative legacies of the aviators.

Pieces of crashed aeroplane were turned into trench art, some of which found a resting place as memory objects in focal positions in the domestic household. Through embodied engagement with the trench art within the space of the home, 'the presence of absence comes to be produced' and felt as the memories of the aviators are retained.[40]

The post-war biographies of First World War aviation-related trench art and/or souvenirs and the way they affected the lives of those living during the interwar years has been conceptualized by Saunders as the 'memory bridge' which, during a period of great social, economic, and cultural change, was 'composed of materiality, emotion and memory . . . accorded shape to peoples' lives as well as their perceptions of the First World War'.[41] Such objects became legacies associated with First World War pilots, bestowing on them a powerful presence today. In reifying the stories imbued within them it is clear that 'objects stimulate remembering, not only through . . . mantelpiece souvenirs, but also by the serendipitous encounter, bringing back experiences which otherwise would have remained dormant, repressed or forgotten'.[42]

The biographies of trench art made from pieces of crashed aeroplane constantly introduce new meanings as new connections with other people and institutions, such as museums, materialize. The social life events identified for each object discussed might include some, but not all, of the following:

(a) pre-acquisition event;
(b) acquisition event;
(c) manufacturing event;
(d) objects of focus in the home of the bereaved;
(e) object of focus in the home of an aviator who survived the war;
(f) object suffers 'social death' as it is stored out of sight in cupboard, garage, attic, or archives);
(g) object 'reactivated' as collector's item for sale as militaria;[43]
(h) museum exhibit;
(i) academic research.

My biographical approach to aviator-related trench art reveals a post-war world where people's front rooms contained trench art and souvenirs of the war as objects of focus. These items became memory objects infused with the stories of the aviators who souvenired them or had them made. They were also objects that drew in a host of other people who might have been involved in their production, in their collection, and, decades later, were involved in their sale or purchase on Internet sites like eBay, in their research, or who might have visited them in a museum.

We cannot assume that all aviation trench art and souvenirs retain memories for some examples are devoid of provenance since the original owners and makers have passed on, leaving only low levels of 'connective memory'. As such, these objects might become repositories for 'anonymous memories'.[44] Though that does not signify an end to their stories or, indeed, that they have no stories at all. One stage in the social lives of souvenirs and trench art is when/if they become museum exhibits, many without (or long since lost) stories attached to them. The meanings of aviator-related objects is constantly evolving and this challenges museums to know how to represent and interpret them.

During my war museum research it became clear that there were many missed opportunities to tell stories infused within exhibits, to show items' significance deriving 'from their associations, not only with other similar items, but with experiences, memories, imagination and a wealth of historical documentation'.[45] Uncovering these stories can be challenging. Dominiek Dendooven reports on the vast quantities of souvenirs from the First World War in Belgian Flanders which are returned to the In Flanders Fields Museum in Ypres following the death of the original owner. He stresses that museum staff should record the stories that accompany an object for it is such stories which bestow value, meaning, and significance.[46] Objects are continually endowed with new meanings and the deposit of trench art in a museum does not necessarily mean the end of its social life, for museums, such as the RAF Museum London and the RAF Museum Cosford, create new exhibitions, breathe new life into their exhibits, and thereby afford the viewing public a renewed sense of the past.

Chapter 11

How Time Flies

The aim of this book was, in part, to portray a more personal, intimate, individual, and emotional interpretation of the relationship between pilots and their aeroplanes and the social worlds they created in the process. The approach also provided a means of documenting and analysing First World War aviation to enhance understanding of human nature and creativity at the limits of human endurance, through exploring issues of materiality, sensoriality, and technology in conflict.

Authenticity

The relativity of the notion of authenticity is an important focus for aviation objects because, as with any objects, they are differently interpreted and valued by different people at different times. Pilot Vernon Castle wrote in a letter to his wife that he had amassed a collection of souvenirs to bring home, some to keep at home and some to give away, recognizing that they would be of great interest to people because they were connected to his wartime experiences and would then be more authentic. This of course raises the issue of the many souvenirs which originally had 'authenticating stories' but which have since lost them – are they any less authentic than those whose stories have survived? Objects with no stories, such as commercially made examples, have no 'authentic' authenticity, but can be ascribed it through fictitious stories which, if believed by others, leaves them perhaps in difficult-to-analyse liminal spaces.

Questions of the contested nature of authenticity become apparent in terms of the consumption of aviation trench art and souvenirs. On the one hand, for example, modern day Parisian collectors view trench art to be authentic only if it was made by soldiers during 1914–18, and not by civilians, such as battlefield pilgrims, internees and refugees, who also experienced the consequences of war.[1] On the other hand, Saunders' definition of trench art is purposely broader, extending to 'any item made by soldiers, prisoners of war and civilians' so long as the they and the trench art can be connected with armed conflict or its consequences.[2]

Pilgrim tourists took their trench-art souvenirs home and this 'displays the romance of contraband, for its scandal is its removal from its "natural" location. Yet, it is only by means of its material relation to that location that it acquires its value'.[3] Since a souvenir may 'authenticate a past . . . experience' this may become troublesome in the future.[4] Future generations, for example, may, perhaps, mistakenly, think that the souvenir trench-art biplane (see Plate 13) had been made by a relative who was a member of the RFC.

It has been suggested that some servicemen may have created or purchased trench art with the aim of promoting a false identity in terms of military experience and achievement (as they undoubtedly did with medals).[5] Such questions relating to the authenticity of a person's war experience would add to the story of the object and therefore change its meaning over time. However, the authenticity of aviators' material culture is of a different order than infantry material culture. It would be very difficult for a 'would-be pilot', as opposed to an infantryman, to fake his identity because the RFC was such a small unit and there were so few pilots that it would have been much easier to identify a 'liar' or a 'fake' pilot than a soldier.

Airmen's writings were first-person experiential descriptions and, therefore, very individual and personal accounts, as their descriptions of particular events could never be exactly the same. Interestingly, the pencil 'endowing the hand with a voice that has more permanence than the speaking voice', such writings also being tangible commemorative legacies of the aviators.[6]

In a catalogue entitled *War in the Sunshine. The British in Italy 1917–1918*, the images contained in the Estorick Collection's exhibition provide interesting points of view on the war in the air.[7] Of particular interest is Jonathan Black's chapter about the fighter pilot and Official War Artist, Sydney Carline.[8] As a witness, Carline painted what he saw and some of the battles he fought in. His paintings were criticized by the Ministry of Information's Royal Air Force sub-Committee who deemed that his depiction of anti-aircraft bursts did not appear convincing which was ironic given that such bursts had nearly shot him down on two occasions.[9] On one occasion, Carline looks at another artist's painting and, standing before 'this sombre and darkly brooding image', 'pondered how different the air war had seemed for him in the skies above Italy, possessing so much more "sun and light and delight"'.[10] Even war artists it seems see and experience the war differently.

The First World War in the air was not just 'a single indisputable legacy' but also 'a heritage that we are all creating and shaping as we come into contact with new and different understandings and presentations of its physical remains, and of the personal experiences' imbued in them.[11]

This book has captured a moment in time, a unique transition between untold millennia of humankind being bound to the earth, and its escape into the heavens in the wood and linen aircraft of the First World War. It is a story of technology, emotion, superstition, courage, skill, and conflict that can never be repeated.

Notes

Prologue
1. It was not possible to fly in a First World War biplane so it was necessary to find an alternative that offered the experience of flying in an open cockpit, exposed to the elements. I chose a 1930s Tiger Moth biplane flying from Duxford airfield, Cambridgeshire.
2. Pink (2009), 64.
3. Lewis (1964), ix.

Chapter 1
1. Granville White (2019), 17.
2. Douglas (1963), 40.
3. Taylor (1968), 11–12.
4. Balfour (1933), 79.
5. Raleigh (1922).
6. Raleigh (1922).
7. Wall (1919), 47.
8. When the Royal Flying Corps became the Royal Air Force, it retained the motto, *per ardua ad astra*.
9. Gould Lee (1969), 23.
10. Connerton (1989).
11. Buchli and Lucas (eds) (2001a), 80.
12. Crawford (1921), (1923), (1929).
13. Flying ace: a pilot who is credited with a number of victories shooting down enemy aircraft during aerial combat. It is not clear how many victories a pilot had to claim to be labelled a flying ace, but as an indicator, Shores et al. only include pilots who achieved five or more victories in their book about flying aces (Shores, Franks and Guest (1990), 6–10, 30). Dogfight: close-flying combat between military aircraft.
14. Anon. j. (1926), 134–5.
15. Taylor (1968), book cover.
16. Wall (1919), 140.
17. Grinnell-Milne (1957 (1933)), 9.
18. Bus: First World War pilot slang for aeroplane. Bott ('Contact') (1918), 11–12.
19. McHardy (2007 (1918)).
20. Bott ('Contact') (1918).
21. Strange (1935), Foreword.

22. Anon. j. (1926), 67.
23. Publication of John McGavock Grider's diary was arranged by his friend Elliott White Springs, *Unknown Aviator*. See Anon. j.
24. Lidsey (1916–17), Private documents. IWM Docs 16504.
25. McCudden (1930 (1918)).
26. Bott ('Contact') (1918).
27. Brancker (1918), Introduction.

Chapter 2

1. Tilley et al. (eds) (2006), 1.
2. Connor (2010), 14, 38, 291, 300.
3. Sloterdijk (2009 (2002)), 9–46.
4. Latour (2006), 105.
5. Sloterdijk (2009 (2002)), 16.
6. Sloterdijk (2009 (2002)), 16.
7. Sloterdijk (2009 (2002)), 19–20.
8. Sloterdijk (2009 (2002)), 9–46.
9. Vinge (1975), 7.
10. Aristotle (1986 (350 BC)), 168–86.
11. Rivlin and Gravelle (1984), 9–28.
12. Howes (1991b), 167–91.
13. Gibson (1986 (1979)).
14. Gibson (1966), 48, 97.
15. Gibson (1986 (1979)).
16. Passing of time, Bergson (2008 (1910)); scale, Lock and Molyneaux (eds) (2006); distance, Helms (1988).
17. Kinaesthesia is the pickup of body and limb movement (muscles and joints).
18. Gosden (2001), 163.
19. Csordas (1994a), 4.
20. Balfour (1933), 76.
21. Anon. j. (1926), 267.
22. Crummy (1983), 139.
23. Gell (1998), 5, 16.
24. Saunders (2003), 11.
25. The Cenotaph is a war memorial, designed by Sir Edward Lutyens, erected in Whitehall, London, in 1920. It was erected initially to remember the victims of the First World War. Today, it more generally commemorates every dead serviceman and woman who has died in every war since and including the First World War.
26. Winter (2006), 104.
27. Saunders (2003), 3.
28. Appadurai (1986a), 3–63.
29. Saunders (2003), 4.
30. Kopytoff (1986), 66–7.
31. Hallam and Hockey (2001).
32. Saunders (2007), 2.

Chapter 3

1. Bott ('Contact') (1918), 221. NB A bull's eye is a hard-boiled sweet.
2. Blériot: French aircraft designed by Louis Blériot and first used by him to make the first flight over the English Channel in 1909. A monoplane, it was produced in both single- and two-seat versions and was purchased by many countries. It was used in the First World War. MacCarron (2006), xi.
3. Lewis (2009 (1936)), 170.
4. Maclennan (2009), 64.
5. MacCarron (2006), 71.
6. Taylor (1968), 30.
7. Wall (1919), 113.
8. Skelton (1977), 62–73.
9. The joystick, also called the control column, can be moved in four directions, left to right and fore and aft. A sideways movement operates the ailerons to control the angle of bank in a turn (the aileron looks like a flap on the lower wing). The fore and aft movement of the stick moves the elevators on either side of the aircraft and are hinged to the rear of the tail-plane, and cause the nose of the machine to go up or down (Thom (1987), 28–9).
10. The rudder controls the direction of the aeroplane and so helps turn the aircraft. To control 'yaw' means to change the horizontal direction in which the aeroplane nose is pointing.
11. Copeland Maltby (1915–16), Personal diary. RAF Museum London, AC73/15/2/5.
12. Taylor (1968), 63.
13. *Ondata zibethicus* (also called muskrat), a large North American rodent with a musky smell, valued for its fur. Taylor (1968), 58.
14. Castle (1919), 162–3.
15. Castle (1919), 192.
16. Taylor (1968), 140.
17. Gould Lee (1969), 99.
18. Montagu (1986 (1971)), 3.
19. Granville White (2019), 37–8.
20. Taylor (1968), 61.
21. McCudden (1930 (1918)), 77.
22. Gould Lee (1969a), 40.
23. Gould Lee (1969), 69.
24. Wing Commander Routh (n.d.), Private documents. IWM Docs 20671.
25. Gould Lee (1969), 60.
26. MacCarron (2006), 145.
27. Downing (1916–17), Private documents. IWM Docs 6.
28. Granville White (2019), 58.
29. Wall (1919), 116.
30. Bott ('Contact') (1918), 140–1.
31. Bott ('Contact') (1918), 141.
32. Bott ('Contact') (1918), 155.

33. Lewis (1964), 83.
34. John William Davies (1987), Interview with John William Davies (recorded and interviewed by Conrad Wood) (IWM Cat. No. 10078).
35. Thom (1987), 132–4.
36. Ortweiler (1917), Private documents. RAF Museum London, AC88/73.
37. Ortweiler (1917), Private documents. RAF Museum London, AC88/73.
38. Gascoyne (1972), Interview with James Gascoyne (IWM Cat. No. 16).
39. Hopkins (1972), 46.
40. The RE8 was a British two-seat reconnaissance and bomber biplane.
41. Gould Lee (1969a), 24.
42. The Albatros was a fighter biplane used by the Imperial German Air Service. There were many variants, e.g., DII, DIII, D5, D5a. The DIII model was particularly favoured by German aircrew for its rate of climb and manoeuvrability even though it was heavy on the controls. Taylor does not state which model of Albatros he flew.
43. Taylor (1968), 116.
44. Kinaesthetic sense: The pickup of body and limb movement (muscles and joints).
45. Taylor (1968), 116.
46. Avro was a British aeroplane manufacturer, founded in 1910. It made the Avro 504, a training aeroplane used in the First World War.
47. Maclennan (2009), 59.
48. Geurts (2002), Loc. 973.
49. Latour (1993), Loc. 565.
50. Vestibular sense: Perception of balance and body position, acceleration and deceleration. Lewis (2009 (1936)), 25.
51. Downing (1916–17), 25, Private documents. IWM Docs 6.
52. Oblique aerial photographs are shot at an angle to reveal details not shown in vertical aerial photographs, e.g. objects under trees may not be visible in vertical aerial photographs. Oblique aerial photographs cover more ground than vertical ones.
53. Castle (1919), 152.
54. Archie: The name given by the British to German anti-aircraft fire: 'Our machines whilst working over the line were frequently shelled by anti-aircraft guns, and it was just about this time that they were nicknamed "Archibalds", probably because they always missed our machines, and the pilots used to sing the refrain of "Archibald! Certainly not!!"' (McCudden (1930 (1918))). Vann (1978), 23.
55. Bott ('Contact') (1918), 91.
56. Rodaway (1994), 26.
57. McCudden (1930 (1918)), 75.
58. Smart (1916–17), Private documents. RAF Museum London, AC98/31/69.

Chapter 4
1. Gould Lee (1969), 41.
2. Lewis (1964), 64.
3. Gould Lee (1969), 50.
4. Howes (1991a), 3–5.

5. Horizon: A visual reference point where the line at which the earth's surface and the sky appear to meet. If a pilot loses sight of the horizon, for example, in poor weather conditions with low or no visibility, he would be unable to determine his body position in space and would therefore experience spatial disorientation.
6. Gibson (1950), 6.
7. Gibson (1986 (1979)), 129.
8. Visual kinaesthesis: An aviator picked up information through head turning and limb movement relative to the body as well as locomotion relative to the environment. Vision is no longer an objectifying sense as a pilot's trained eyes must periodically focus on the horizon as he scans the larger environment ahead, to verify attitude (Gibson (1986 (1979)), 126). Interestingly, Gibson's seminal contributions to this topic were greatly influenced by his Second World War work on the effect of flying on visual perception.
9. Lewis (2009 (1936)), 175.
10. Compston (2009 (1931)), 87–8.
11. Tyro: Inexperienced pilot.
12. Wortley (1982 (1928)), 165–6.
13. Battle of the Somme, 1 July–13 November 1916.
14. Evans (1921), 3–4.
15. Vertical aerial photographs are shot from immediately above the subject of the image being photographed – produces a flat map-like image.
16. Gould Lee (1969), 68.
17. Douglas (1963), 133.
18. Yuille (1973) (IWM Cat. No. 4267).
19. Lewis (1964), 74.
20. Seremetakis (1994), 9.
21. Lewis (1964), 75.
22. Yuille (1973) (IWM Cat. No. 4267).
23. Classen (2012), 123.
24. Ward-Jackson (ed.) (1945), 22.
25. Nettleingham (1917), 76.
26. Gould Lee (1969a), 128.
27. Wall (1919), 115.
28. Gould Lee (1969), 46.
29. Taylor (1968), 28.
30. Gould Lee (1969), 186.
31. Winterton (2012), 230. See also Scarry (1985), 255.
32. Ortweiler (1917). Private documents. RAF Museum London, AC88/73.
33. Bott ('Contact') (1918), 96.
34. Maclennan (2009), 59.
35. Maclennan (2009), 59.
36. Ortweiler (1917). Private documents. RAF Museum London, AC88/73.
37. Hart (2005), 108.
38. Bott ('Contact') (1918), 10.

39. Bott ('Contact') (1918), 18.
40. Verey lights were a type of flare gun fired at night.
41. Anon. j. (1926), 160–1.
42. Compston (2009 (1931)), 85.
43. Davies (1987), Interview (IWM Cat. No. 10078).
44. By late 1917, aviators communicated by wireless with artillery battalions on the ground. Both voice over wireless (radio telephony) and Morse code over wireless (wireless telegraphy) was used (Bruton (2016)).
45. Davies (1987), Interview (IWM Cat. No. 10078).
46. Copeland Maltby (1915–16), Personal diary. RAF Museum London, AC73/15/2/5.
47. Rodaway (1994), 32.
48. The term 'distributed persons' is an interesting concept for which anthropologist Alfred Gell uses the example of Pol Pot's mine-laying soldiers in Cambodia whose mines-as-weapons were part of their 'distributed personhood', wherever they were geographically, and thus were the 'objective embodiments of the power or capacity to will their use' (Gell (1998), 20–1, 222). A challenging extension of this can be applied to an aviator as he was instrumental in causing events to happen in areas far removed spatially from where his body, flying thousands of feet above the earth, was currently located.
49. Wall (1919), 115.
50. Maclennan (2009), 59.
51. Hopkins (1972), 45–57, 48.
52. MacCarron (2006), 84–5.
53. Anon. j. (1926), 173.
54. Anon. j. (1926), 168.
55. Anon. j. (1926), 168–9.
56. Lewis (1964), vii.
57. Aldis collimation sight: A sealed metal tube, 32in long, 2in in diameter, mounted between the Sopwith Camel's two Vickers guns. The internal lenses of these sights secured an image in the ratio of 1:1, thus images were neither reduced nor magnified, i.e., it is not a telescopic sight. Two concentric rings engraved on the glass were used to give an estimate of the distance to the target aimed at with the inner 100yd ring being a guide as to when to open fire.
58. Ralph (1999), 81–2.
59. Kemp (2000), 150.
60. Motor car mascots, such as metal dogs and cats, were fitted on to car radiators and 'carried for fun rather than genuine amulets' (Wright and Lovett (1908), 292).
61. Morris et al. (1981), 219–20.
62. Morris et al. (1981), 30.
63. German pilot Manfred von Richthofen, also known as the Red Baron, was a fighter pilot in the German Air Service and considered to be a flying ace. He originally joined the war as a member of the cavalry, but then transferred to the Air Service in 1915 where he rapidly distinguished himself. One of Germany's national heroes, he was killed during the First World War in April 1918. He has been the subject of many books and films.

64. Strange (1935), 175–8.
65. Lewis (2009 (1936)), 148.
66. Geldard (1953), 266.
67. Lewis (2009 (1936)), 56.
68. Strange (1935), 81.
69. As the speed increases, the sound of the wind on the external wires holding the aeroplane's wings to the fuselage and to each other would change both in pitch and loudness. The wires have a natural frequency of oscillation which would change due to the wind friction upon them.
70. Due to increased gravitational forces and pressures exerted on the body.
71. Side-slipping: The act of banking in one direction using the ailerons and the rudder in opposite direction simultaneously. This causes the aeroplane to slip sideways left or right of the main longitudinal direction of travel and would cause an apparent wind on the face opposite to the direction of slip (Thom (1987), 132–4). Strange (1935), 81.
72. Strange (1935), 81–2.
73. Csordas (1994a), 4.
74. Csordas (1994a), 1–24, 25.
75. Thrift (2010), 639.
76. Scarry (1985), 255.
77. Rodaway (1994), 32.
78. Geurts (2002), Loc. 973.

Chapter 5
1. Captain F. Williams (2019), 140–1.
2. Wyschogrod (1981), 25–43; Paterson (2007), Loc. 386.
3. Gould Lee (1969a), 53–4.
4. Dunn (1941), 2.
5. Anon. j. (1926), 276.
6. Waite (ed.) (2012 (1979)), 732.
7. Armstrong-Jones (1929), 135–6.
8. Waite (ed.) (2012 (1979)), 444.
9. Villiers (1929), 10.
10. Sharper Knowlson (1934 (1910)), 155.
11. Paine (2004), 10.
12. Wright and Lovett (1908), 289.
13. Animals were popular squadron mascots and regularly appear in photographs of air and ground crew. Many of these images feature a wide variety of animals, e.g., lion, dog, monkey, fox, pig, and fighting cock, kept by RFC squadrons and individual aviators. Although I have omitted including them in this book, such information may provide a worthwhile area of research in the future for it is an interesting, yet under-researched, area of modern conflict and would make a useful comparison to the lucky mascot animal objects which, though non-living, could be perceived as spiritually active 'creatures'.
14. Wright and Lovett (1908), 288.
15. Sharper Knowlson (1934 (1910)), 157.

16. The word 'mascot' 'covers luck-bringing persons as well as objects, appears to have been derived from a Provençal word *mascotte* popularised by Andran's comic opera "L Mascott", which was first performed at the end of 1880. The word *mascot* originally meant a gambler's "fetish", and was used in the patois of Marseilles, where Andran was born' (Wright and Lovett (1908), 289).
17. Bratley (1907), 61.
18. Villiers (1929), 36–7, 90, 120, 160–1.
19. Villiers (1929), 9.
20. The Sacred Heart badge was an oval piece of red cloth bearing the representation of Christ, which was sewn inside the tunic (Turner (1980), 138).
21. Turner (1980), 138–9.
22. Wall (1919), 203.
23. Amateur folklorist Edward Lovett (1852–1933) hailed from Croydon in Surrey. Over the years he amassed an impressive collection of thousands of mascots and charms. As a member of the council of the Folklore Society, he often wrote for the Society's journal. He developed relationships with many museums, primarily as a means of selling objects to them but also to publicize his work.
24. Lovett (1925), 15.
25. Lovett (1928), 3.
26. Lovett (1925), 72.
27. Bratley (1907).
28. Anon. j. (1926), 140.
29. Bratley (1907), 146.
30. Ortweiler (1917). Private documents. RAF Museum London, AC88/73.
31. Military bugle/trumpet calls have been used by the armed forces for centuries as a means of communication and, perhaps the best known of all bugle calls is the last post. This marks the end of the day and is also sounded to show respect for the dead at funerals.
32. Gould Lee (1969), 41.
33. National Museum of Wales website, museum.wales/collections/online/?field0=string&value0=edward lovett collection mascots&field1=with_images&value1=on&page=1.
34. Turner (1980), 38.
35. Becker (1998), 96–103.
36. Fussell (2000 (1975)), 124.
37. Hill (2007), 78.
38. The black cat was considered to be lucky, an old and equally modern superstition (Sharper Knowlson (1934 (1910)), 185). Villiers (1929), 36–7.
39. Chambers (2004), 79–102.

Chapter 6
1. Wright and Lovett (1908), 288–303.
2. Rose O'Neill (1874–1944) published cartoons of Kewpies in, for example, the *Ladies Home Journal* and *Good Housekeeping* (Formanek-Brunell (ed.) (1997)).
3. Wall (1919), 47.
4. See Tuck DB Postcards, History of R. Tuck and Sons Ltd. http://tuckdb.org/history

5. Villiers (1929), 161.
6. Morris et al. (1981), 191.
7. Roud (2006), 484.
8. MacDonagh (1916), 269.
9. Castle (1919), 142.
10. John Bull is a fictitious epitomist of Englishness and British imperialism, popularized by British print makers; originally the creation of Dr John Arbuthnot in 1712 (*Oxford Dictionary of National Biography*, www.oxforddnb.com/view/article/68195?docPos=3).
11. It is believed that the finder of a four-leaf clover will be fortunate, and an old country rhyme says of a four-leaf clover: 'One leaf for fame, And one leaf for wealth, And one for a faithful lover, And one to bring you glorious health, Are all in a four leaf clover' (Villiers (1929), 40). MacDonagh (1916), 268.
12. The True Cross is a Christian relic and reputed to be the wood of the cross on which Jesus Christ was crucified.
13. Australian War Memorial Museum website (Marston), www.awm.gov.au/collection/REL33983.
14. Appadurai (1986a), 3–63.
15. Poulbot (1917).
16. Hand of Fatima: Perceived as a symbol of strength and power (Wallis Budge (1968), 467). Scarab beetle: Dung-eating beetle. Collecting a mass of dung, the beetle lays one egg in it. The beetle then kneads the dung into a ball. It then rolls the ball along the ground and out into the sunshine; such action being compared to the sun's progress across the sky. The heat of the sun enables the egg to hatch and the new beetle lives and thrives on the dung within which the egg has been surrounded. Since earliest times the Egyptians have associated this type of beetle with the god of creation, and its egg-ball with the sun. They wore models of the beetle, in the form of scarab amulets, when living to afford them the life and strength of the god of creation (Thomas and Pavitt (1914), 67); Wallis Budge (1968), 135–6. Poulbot (1917).
17. Lloyd Sproule (1917–18), Private documents. RAF Museum London, AC97/69/22.
18. Anon. j. (1926), 276.
19. Seremetakis (1994a), 9.
20. 'Beatrice Lillie': date of birth 20.05.1894–20.01.1989. Canadian born British comedic performer, actress, and singer. Made her first West End debut in 1914.
21. G. Crutchley (u.d.), 'My grandfather'. www.flyingclothing.co.uk/pg005.html.
22. Villiers (1929), 157.
23. War History Online, www.warhistoryonline.com/war-articles/relatives-red-baron-albert-ball-meetroyal-air-force-museum.html.
24. Fitzsimons (2010), 109.
25. Lovett (1928), 3.
26. Hildburgh (1951), 238.
27. Taylor (1968), 62.
28. Anon. j. (1926), 276.

29. Anon. e. (1915), 3.
30. Whilst in Western empirical scientific thought it is not possible for objects to be magical by themselves, Alfred Gell, in *Art and Agency*, promotes the idea of the agency of things where '*persons* or "social agents" are, in certain contexts, substituted for by *art objects*' (Gell (1998), 5). For Gell an agent was one who 'causes events to happen' and 'whenever an event is believed to happen because of an intention lodged in the person or thing which initiates the causal sequence, that is an instance of agency' (Gell (1998), 5, 16). This idea is especially useful in my analysis of the agency of magic and folklore in lucky mascots because it is less what an art object represents than what it does within the social world of the aviators that has significance.
31. Anon. e. (1915), 3.
32. Loraine (1938), 186, 189.
33. This is a poem by the poet William Wordsworth which describes the ideal man in arms. Composed in 1806, following the death of Lord Nelson, and first published in 1807, it asks 'Who is the happy Warrior? Who is he that every man in arms should wish to be?' (Wordsworth (1984 (1807))).
34. Loraine (1938), 217.
35. McCudden (1930 (1918)), 189.
36. Anon. e. (1915), 3.
37. McCudden (1930 (1918)), 204.
38. Baring (1920), 283–4.
39. Saunders (2003), 163.
40. Skelton (1979), 114–20.

Chapter 7

1. Anon. j. (1926), 89.
2. 'McScotch' (1985 (1936)), 81.
3. Dunn (1941), 2.
4. Paine (2004), 10.
5. Brokensha (2008), 2–6.
6. Taylor (1968), 126–7.
7. Macmillan (2015 (1929)).
8. Gould Lee (1969), 131.
9. Gould Lee (1969), 193.
10. 'Go west': be killed.
11. Grinnell-Milne (1957 (1933)), 21, 125.
12. Macmillan (2015 (1929)).
13. Hertz (1973 (1909)), 3–31.
14. Roud (2006), 444.
15. *Feng shui* means wind and water, both of which flow. *Qi* is the cosmic energy and there are two types – *Sheng Qi* is auspicious and brings life; *Xie Qui* is ominous and brings death (Ruan (1996), 217–18).
16. Hertz (1973 (1909)), 12.

17. Anthropological interpretation of peoples' actions provides interesting observations. For example, Bourdieu explores the lived domestic environment of an Algerian Kabyle House in *The World Reversed*, introducing *habitus* concepts in terms of a series of binary oppositions that structured the occupants' lives. In particular, he observes how the hearth is the site of a number of rites and that 'the fireplace and the stones surrounding it derive their magical power, whether to give protection from the evil eye or illness or to bring fine weather, from the fact that they belong to the order of fire, the dry, and the heat of the sun'. For example, rites used to effect a change in the weather utilize opposing parts of the house differentiating between the wet or dry part of the house. To change the weather from wet to dry, a wool-packing comb made from fire along with a glowing ember are left on the threshold overnight. The direction that the house faced was of importance too with the front door of the main house in which the head of the family resided having an east orientation (Bourdieu (1979), 144). Similarly, individuals performed actions in accordance with cardinal orientation in order to achieve a particular favourable outcome just as First World War pilots developed ways of behaving in an attempt to survive the war.
18. Dunn (1941), 2.
19. Strenski (1992 (1922)), 35.
20. Dunn (1941), 2.
21. Roud (2006), 342.
22. The origin of it being unlucky to sit thirteen to a table may stem from the Last Supper where thirteen were present and the tragedies subsequent to that meal may be re-enacted on any occasion when thirteen are seated at a table (Sharper Knowlson (1934 (1910)), 168–9). Macmillan (2015 (1929)).
23. Taylor (1968), 119–21.
24. Bell (1992), 3–7.
25. Villiers (1929), 90.
26. RAF London Museum, Accession No. 80c991.
27. Maurice Farman biplane: Shorthorn and Longhorn. Used as a reconnaissance and light bomber aircraft during the early part of the First World War. It was later used as a training aeroplane.
28. See Mauss (1990 (1954)).
29. Taylor (1968), 120–1.
30. Anon. d. (1917).
31. Gell (1998), 16.
32. Bott ('Contact') (1918), 212.
33. Dunn (1941), 2.
34. Henry Allingham (1896–2009) was the oldest surviving veteran of the First World War. He was 113 years' old when he died (Allingham with Goodwin (2009)).
35. Allingham with Goodwin (2009), 101.
36. Lawson and Lawson (1996), 147–8.
37. St Christopher was a third-century martyr. He was the patron saint of travellers as well as being invoked against sudden death. It was believed that whoever saw an image of St Christopher would not die that day (Farmer (2011), 89–90).

Notes   135

38. Castle (1919), 134, 137.
39. Castle (1919), 142.
40. The rotary engines of early aircraft threw out a fine spray of castor oil. Castor oil emits a very recognizable smell and was the preferred lubricant for rotary engines during the First World War. It is known to be an effective laxative and could cause a pilot problems if too much was accidently ingested during flight.
41. Castle (1919), 88–9.
42. Loraine (1938), 216.
43. Bible Gateway Psalm 91, www.biblegateway.com/passage/?search=Psalm+91&version=KJV. These words come from the King James Version – the English translation of the Christian Bible for the Church of England (other versions cite the Psalm quite differently in places). The King James Bible was the mainspring of religious cultural life during the First World War (Snape and Parker (2001), 404).
44. Wall (1919), 178.
45. Ashton (1917), 6, 8–13.
46. Turner (1980), 139.
47. Becker (1998), 97, quoted from Roure (1917), 710–11.
48. Frazer (1994 (1911)), 46.
49. Tarlow (2000), 728, 713.
50. Saunders (1999), 243.
51. Witnessing soldiers' experiences in the First World War, French sociologist Marcel Mauss became aware that the human body had to be trained (habituated) in the use of a variety of technologies (however simple), and that this only came through experience. Mauss gives the example of the apparently simple use of a spade to dig trenches and dugouts. The English troops he accompanied did not know how to dig with a French spade and, on occasions when a French division was relieved by an English one, or vice versa, 8,000 spades had to be changed, illustrating that techniques and skills need to be learnt (Mauss (1979 (1935)), 99).
52. Malinowski (2015 (1922)), Locs. 2528, 2535.
53. Lewis (2009 (1936)), 154.
54. Clark (1999 (1973)), 92.
55. Mauss (1990 (1954)).
56. Pels (2010), 613–33, 614.
57. Watson (2006), 249.

Chapter 8

1. Wall (1919), 113.
2. Grinnell-Milne (1957 (1933)), 200.
3. Tarlow (1999), 25, 35.
4. Hallam and Hockey (2001), 86.
5. Established by Royal Charter on 21 May 1917, the Commonwealth War Graves Commission honours the 1.7 million men and women of the Commonwealth forces who died in the First and Second World Wars, and ensures that they will never be forgotten. The Commission's principles are: (1) each of the dead should be commemorated by

name on the headstone or memorial; (2) headstones/memorials should be permanent; (3) headstones should be uniform; and (4) no distinction should be made on account of military rank, race, or creed, CWGC (Commonwealth War Graves Commission): 'About Us' www.cwgc.org/about-us.
6. Kopytoff (1986).
7. Souveniring: servicemen obsessed with finding souvenirs and trophies of war.
8. University of Sydney, Roll of Service, p. 215, http://beyond1914.sydney.edu.au/profile/3126/john-hay.
9. Jasta 11: No. 11 Fighter Squadron (German). Australian War Memorial Museum website, (Hay): www.awm.gov.au/collection/C289714.
10. Franks et al. (2007), 53–4.
11. University of Sydney, Roll of Service, p. 215, http://beyond1914.sydney.edu.au/profile/3126/john-hay.
12. Australian War Memorial Museum website (Hay), www.awm.gov.au/collection/C289714.
13. Douglas (1963), 171.
14. Douglas (1963), 320–1.
15. Parachutes were, however, discussed at the Royal Aircraft Factory, particularly Calthrop's 'Guardian Angel' (AIR 1/1121/204/5/20731. December 1916 – 2 February 1918, Reports on 'Guardian Angel' type of parachute) and tests were successfully carried out on the Calthrop parachute in 1917 (AIR 5/1348. 1917, Tests of E.R. Calthrop's 'Guardian Angel' parachute, Type A). There was, however, no British order for free-fall parachutes until September 1918 (by this time the RFC and RNAS had combined to form the RAF). Parachutes were simply not adopted by the British Army for aeroplane pilots and their observers.
16. Strange (1935), 216.
17. Douglas (1963), 321.
18. Jones (ed.) (1934), 149.
19. 'McScotch' (1985 (1936)), 88.
20. The BE aeroplane was used by the RFC during the First World War for reconnaissance duties, particularly artillery observation and aerial photography.
21. Grinnell-Milne (1957 (1933)), 69.
22. Orpen (1921), 53–4.
23. Arkell (1918), Private documents. IWM documents (online) 6706/G and H. Available from: www.iwm.org.uk/collections/item/object/103003125.
24. Lewis (1964), 56.
25. Indeed, Bourdieu's concept of *habitus* recognized that objects help people learn how to act appropriately (see Bourdieu (1977)), thereby apportioning substance to the idea that objects make people (see, e.g. Miller (1998a)).
26. Anon. f. (1918), 108.
27. Nieuport Scout: French-built, single-seater fighter biplane, first built in 1916, deemed to have a good rate of climb.
28. Leslie (ed.) (1924), 199–200.
29. Leslie (ed.) (1924), 199–200.

30. Leslie (ed.) (1924), 231–2.
31. Campion Vaughan (1981), 113.
32. Williams (2019), 183.
33. MacCarron (2006), 166–7.
34. Commonwealth War Graves Commission: Corbett Wilson and Woodiwiss, www.cwgc.org/find-war-dead/casualty/585327/corbett-wilson,- denys/#&gid=null&pid=1.
35. Granville White (2019), 40–1.
36. Williamson (2009 (1929)), Loc. 1048–1052.
37. Lloyd (1998).
38. Hallam and Hockey (2001), 173.
39. Lloyd (1998), Loc. 2226.
40. Anon. g. (1918), 1094.
41. Walton (2010).
42. Seton Hutchison (1936), 1, 194.
43. Pulteney and Brice (1925).
44. Jünger (2004 (1920)), 261.
45. A Cross of Sacrifice was erected in most CWGC cemeteries. Designed by architect Reginald Blomfeld, it was a stone cross with a symbolic sword of bronze attached to its face – this emphasized the military character of the cemetery as well as the religious affiliation of most of the dead (Longworth (2010 (1967)), 36).
46. Buchli and Lucas (eds) (2001a), 80.
47. The Battle of Arras, 9 April–16 May 1917, also termed 'Bloody April', resulted in huge casualties for the RFC, largely due to the Germans having the upper hand in terms of air superiority – their Albatros fighter aeroplane was more technologically advanced than the British fighter aeroplanes.
48. Saunders (2002a), 177.
49. Holt and Holt (1996).
50. Stewart (1993), 134.
51. Stewart (1993), 135.
52. Hammerton (ed.) (1914), 431.
53. Hammerton (ed.) (1914), 431.
54. Such trench art can be attributed to Saunders' sub-category 2b, i.e., made by civilians after the war during 1919–39 (Saunders (2003), 45–9).
55. Pulteney and Brice (1925), 3.
56. Baring (1920), 222.
57. A memorial in Ypres, Belgium, dedicated to the 54,000 soldiers who died in the Ypres Salient before 16 August 1917 and who have no known grave (CWGC: Menin Gate, www.cwgc.org/find/find-cemeteries-and-memorials/91800/ypres-memorial).
58. Gordon (1986), 139.
59. Saunders (2004a), 10.
60. Stewart (1993), 139.
61. Gell (1977), 27.
62. 'The Returned from the Front' website, http://thereturned.co.uk/the-grave-markers/.
63. Pulteney and Brice (1925), 53.

64. Esquelbecq is a village in France, near the Belgian front, some 24km south of Dunkirk.
65. Saunders (2014), 28.
66. 'A Church near you' website, www.achurchnearyou.com/twineham-st-peter/.
67. Saunders (2001), 477.
68. Anon. c. (1917).
69. Colonel Cartwright was, until late 2019, Chairman of Trustees of the museum, but remains Curator of the Collection. Pers. comm. Col. Stamford Cartwright: 7 September 2017 and 22 July 2021.
70. Hallam and Hockey (2001), 85–7.
71. Hallam and Hockey (2001), 213.
72. Hallam and Hockey (2001), 124.
73. Hallam and Hockey (2001), 124.
74. Hallam and Hockey (2001), 124.
75. Bourdieu (1977).
76. Hallam and Hockey (2001), 87.
77. Hallam and Hockey (2001), 77.
78. Hallam and Hockey (2001), 19.
79. Buchli (2002a), 18–19.
80. Hoskins (2006), 78.

Chapter 9

1. 'A thing that is kept as a reminder of a person, place, or event' (Waite (ed.) (2012 (1979)), 697).
2. Grinnell-Milne (1957 (1933)), 162–3.
3. Saunders (2003), 4. Hoskins (1998), 7.
4. Gwinnell (1919), 46.
5. Taylor (1968), 138–9.
6. Gwinnell (1919), 47.
7. Balfour (1933), 96.
8. Baring (1920), 103.
9. McCudden (1930 (1918)), 200.
10. Gould Lee (1969a), 176.
11. Anon. h. (1918), 609.
12. Anthony Arkell (1918), Private documents. IWM documents (online) 6706/G and H. Available from: www.iwm.org.uk/collections/item/object/1030031255.
13. McCudden (1930 (1918)), 200.
14. Wenzel and Cornish (1980), 6.
15. Wenzel and Cornish (1980), 8.
16. Grinnell-Milne (1957 (1933)), 89.
17. Morane Saulnier BB biplane: Reconnaissance two-seater aircraft produced in France in 1915 for the RFC. McCudden (1930 (1918)), 68.
18. The Battle of Messines Ridge, 7 June–14 June 1917, took place on the Western Front near the village of Messines, West Flanders, Belgium.
19. McHardy (2007 (1918)), 166–7.
20. Salvo: Shooting of several guns at the same time in a battle.

21. McHardy (2007 (1918)), 85–6.
22. Nieuport Scout: French-built, single-seater fighter biplane, first built in 1916, deemed to have a good rate of climb.
23. 'McScotch' (1985 (1936)), 89. Books written by servicemen and published both during and immediately after the war were anonymized. Often these books were written using their diaries, and, since it was forbidden for all servicemen to keep a diary or a journal, this made them contested objects.
24. Erected in the Amiens Cemetery, Arras, France. Unveiled by Lord Trenchard, Marshal of the Royal Air Force, on 31 July 1932. It commemorates 1,000 airmen from RFC, RAF, and RNAS forces of the Commonwealth who were killed on the Western Front during the First World War and who have no known grave. Arras was the scene of heavy losses at the Battle of Arras, 1917, also termed 'Bloody April'.
25. McHardy (2007 (1918)), 275.
26. Sopwith Camel: Single-seat biplane fighter aircraft, introduced to the Western Front in 1917.
27. Macmillan (2015 (1929)).
28. *Drachen* observation balloon: A German observation balloon used to spy on Allied soldiers. They hung swinging from the sky whilst attached to a cable which was, in turn, attached to the ground, usually via a motor truck. An observer in one of these balloons can see for at least a 10-mile radius. Though not easily manoeuvrable, and providing a very large target, many pilots experienced frustration as they found it very difficult to hit them with gunfire. Morane Saulnier BB biplane: Reconnaissance two-seater aircraft produced in France in 1915 for the RFC.
29. Macmillan (2015 (1929)).
30. Sopwith Strutter: Used by the RFC from December 1915, this aeroplane was a single- or two-seater fighter biplane. It was described as a 'strutter' because of the arrangement of its central mainplane bracing struts.
31. Macmillan (2015 (1929)).
32. Hallam and Hockey (2001), 8.
33. Anon. j. (1926), 124.
34. Grinnell-Milne (1957 (1933)), 89.
35. Seton Hutchison (1936), 255–6.
36. Cook (2003), 48.
37. Saunders (2003), 49–50.
38. Stewart (1993), 135.
39. Castle (1919), 203–4.
40. Saunders (2003), 49–51.
41. Strafe: The military practice of attacking ground targets with a machine gun from low-flying aircraft.
42. Castle (1919), 203–4.

Chapter 10

1. To put linen into perspective, flax to make the linen skin of First World War aircraft was initially imported from Belgium but later most came from Ireland. Interestingly throughout the First World War, cultivation of flax in Ireland increased from

40,000 acres to 150,000 acres. Irish Linen Centre & Lisburn Museum: Aerolinen – The War was Won on Ulster Wings, www.lisburnmuseum.com/2014/08/the-war-was-won-on-ulster-linen-wings-howaerolinen-and-andrews-mill-in-comber-aided-the-war-effort/.
2. Saunders (2003), 11.
3. Aviation archive (u.d.) Women Doping Wings, www.aviationarchive.org.uk/Gpages/html/G2083.html.
4. Velasco (2010), 8.
5. Raleigh (1922).
6. Heraldry: The 'systematic hereditary use of an arrangement of charges or devices on a shield' and came into being in the mid-twelfth century over a wide area of Europe. Such depiction of arms on a shield imparted a message from individual knights and was held to be a form of vanity and display rather than a practical military device. It was a military status symbol popularized by the tournaments that knights took part in (Woodcock and Robinson (2001 (1988)), 1–3).
7. Grinnell-Milne (1957 (1933)), 204.
8. Grinnell-Milne (1957 (1933)), 190.
9. Grinnell-Milne (1957 (1933)), 205.
10. Langham (2016), Loc. 2638.
11. Pers. comm. RAF Museum London, 6 April 2017.
12. Ralph (1999), 81, 141.
13. Kill: Shooting down or forcing an enemy aeroplane to land although not necessarily killing German aircrew. Ralph (1999), 81.
14. Ralph (1999), 81.
15. Ralph (1999), 141.
16. *Windsock International*: A magazine for First World War aeroplane enthusiasts and scale modellers.
17. See the *Methuen Handbook of Colour* – a universal handbook for people who need to identify and recreate colour (Kornerup and Wanscher (1978)).
18. Roberts (2003).
19. Anon. a. (1918).
20. Anon. a. (1918).
21. Shores et al. (1990), 63.
22. Gould Lee (1969), 64.
23. Pers. comm. RAF Museum London, 6 April 2017.
24. Klee (ed.) (1964), 346.
25. D'Alto (2016).
26. Klee (ed.) (1964), 363.
27. Rewald (1988), 28, 74.
28. Klee (ed.) (1964), 387.
29. Rewald (1988), 98.
30. Cardinal (1994), 72.
31. Anon. b. (n.d.), Interpretation Board. Second Lieutenant Frank Wayman Ely: Trench art biplanes (Shuttleworth Collection) (visited 4 July 2017).

32. Saunders (2009), 49.
33. The Armistice was signed between the Allies of the First World War and Germany for the cessation of hostilities on the Western Front. It was signed at 11 am, 11 November 1918, ending the war but beginning its aftermath.
34. Saunders (2009), 43.
35. Saunders (2009), 46.
36. Saunders (2003), 46.
37. Kimball (2004), 159.
38. The Chinese Labour Corps comprised 135,000 Chinese workers recruited by the British government during the First World War. They were employed from 1916–22 to undertake support work and manual labour in order to free up troops for the front line on the Western Front. They were employed in ports to unload/load cargoes, lay railway lines, repair roads, and construct aerodromes (Fawcett (2000), 42); as well as dig trenches, fill sandbags, and repair tanks and artillery (O'Neill (2016), Loc. 29). Fawcett (2000), 42; Saunders (2012a).
39. Brandon (2000), 18.
40. Hallam and Hockey (2001), 84.
41. Saunders (2001), 477–8.
42. Kwint (1999), 2.
43. Hallam and Hockey (2001), 8.
44. Saunders (2002), 181–206, 199.
45. Saunders and Cornish (2009a), 4.
46. Dendooven (2009), 66.

Chapter 11

1. Isyanova (2009), 142.
2. Saunders (2003), 11.
3. Stewart (1993), 135.
4. Saunders (2003), 139.
5. Saunders (2016), 13.
6. Scarry (1985), 254.
7. Anon. i. (ed.) (2017), *War in the Sunshine. The British in Italy 1917–1918.* Exhibition 13 January–19 March at the Estorick Collection of Modern Italian Art, 39a Canonbury Square, London, N1 2AN.
8. Black (2017).
9. Black (2017), 27.
10. Black (2017), 28.
11. Saunders (2007), 177.

Bibliography

Allingham, H. with D. Goodwin (2009), *Kitchener's Last Volunteer. The Life of Henry Allingham, the Oldest Veteran of the Great War* (Edinburgh: Mainstream Publishing Company).
Anon. a. (1918), *London Gazette (Second Supplement)*, Friday, 29 November, 14203–14204 (London: Her Majesty's Stationery Office).
Anon. b. (n.d.), Interpretation Board. Second Lieutenant Frank Wayman Ely: Trench art biplanes (Shuttleworth Collection) (visited 4 July 2017).
Anon. c. (1917), *Bromsgrove, Droitwich and Redditch Weekly Messenger*, 19 May.
Anon. d. (1917), 'Wonder Boy of the Flying Corps. Missing Airman Who Had 42 Victims. Fight in Pyjamas', *Weekly Despatch*, Sunday, 2 May.
Anon. e. (1915), 'Aviators' Lucky Emblems', *Burra Record* (SA: 187–1954), Wednesday, 17 February, p. 3 (online). Available from: http://nla.gov.au/nla.news-article39037349.
Anon. f. (1918), Personals. *Flight Magazine*, 24 January, p. 108.
Anon. g. (1918), Personals. *Flight Magazine*, 26 September, p. 1094 (online). Available from: www.flightglobal.com/pdfarchive/view/1918/1918%20-%201094.html?search=guy Ashwin.
Anon. h. (1918), 'Awards for Bringing down Gothas', *Flight Magazine*, 6 June, p. 609 (online). Available from: www.flightglobal.com/pdfarchive/view/1918/1918%20- %200611.html?search=anthony arkell.
Anon. i. (ed.) (2017), *War in the Sunshine. The British in Italy 1917–1918*. Exhibition 13 January–19 March 2017 (London: Estorick Foundation).
Anon. j. (1926), *War Birds. Diary of an Unknown Aviator* (New York: George H. Doran Company).
Appadurai, A. (ed.) (1986), *The Social Life of Things. Commodities in cultural perspective* (Cambridge: Cambridge University Press).
—— (1986a), 'Introduction: commodities and the politics of value', in A. Appadurai (ed.), *The Social Life of Things. Commodities in cultural perspective* (Cambridge: Cambridge University Press), pp. 3–63.
Aristotle, (1986 (350 BC)), *De Anima (On the Soul)*, tr. H. Lawson-Tancred (London: Penguin Books).
Arkell, Anthony (1918), Private documents. IWM documents (online) 6706/G and H. Available from: www.iwm.org.uk/collections/item/object/103003125.
Armstrong-Jones, Sir R. (1929), 'Superstition', *Proceedings of the Royal Society of Medicine* (online), 23(2): 135–41. Available from: http://journals.sagepub.com/doi/pdf/10.1177/003591572902300236.

Ashton, H. (1917), 'Prayer shops', *Daily Mail*, 17 January.
Balfour, H.H. (1933), *An Airman Marches* (London: Hutchinson & Co. (Publishers) Ltd).
Baring, M. (1920), *RFC, HQ 1914–1918* (London: G. Bell and Sons).
Becker, A. (1998), *War and Faith: The Religious Imagination in France, 1914–1930 (Legacy of the Great War)* (Oxford: Berg).
Bell, C. (1992), *Ritual Theory. Ritual Practice* (New York (NY): Oxford University Press Inc.).
Bergson, H. (2008 (1910)), *Time and Free Will. An Essay on the Immediate Data of Consciousness* (New York (NY): Cosimo Classics).
Black, J. (2017), '"At the sublime edge of death". Sydney Carline (1888–1929): Fighter Pilot and Official War Artist in Italy, 1918', in Anon. i. (ed.), *War in Sunshine. The British in Italy 1917–1918*. Exhibition 13 January–19 March 2017 (London: Estorick Foundation), 18–32.
Boivin, N. (2008), *Material Cultures, Material Minds. The Impact of Things on Human Thought, Society, and Evolution* (Cambridge: Cambridge University Press).
Bott, A. ('Contact') (1918), *An Airman's Outings* (Edinburgh and London: William Blackwood and Sons).
Bourdieu, P. (1977), *Outline of a Theory of Practice*, tr. R. Nice (Cambridge: Cambridge University Press).
—— (1979), *Algeria 1960. The disenchantment of the world. The sense of honour, the Kabyle house or the world reversed*, tr. R. Nice (Cambridge, London, and New York (NY): Cambridge University Press).
Bourne, J., P. Liddle and I. Whitehead (eds) (2001), *The Great World War 1914–45, Volume 2 The peoples' experience* (London: HarperCollins Publishers).
Brancker, Major General W.S. (1918), 'Introduction', in A. Bott ('Contact') (1918), *An Airman's Outings* (Edinburgh and London: William Blackwood and Sons).
Brandon, S. (2000), *Buttonhooks and Shoehorns* (Princes Risborough: Shire Publications Ltd).
Bratley, G.H. (1907), *The Power of Gems and Charms* (London: Gay & Bird).
Brokensha, H. (2008), 'Prologue – December 1917', in J. Levine, *On a Wing and a Prayer* (London: Collins), pp. 2–6.
Bruton, E. (2016), 'Signalling at the Battle of Passchendaele, July to November 1917' (http://blogs.mhs.ox.ac.uk/innovatingincombat/).
Buchli, V. (ed.) (2002), *The material culture reader* (Oxford and New York (NY): Berg).
—— (2002a), 'Introduction', in V. Buchli (ed.), *The material culture reader* (Oxford and New York (NY): Berg), 1–22.
Buchli, V. and G. Lucas (eds) (2001), *Archaeologies of the Contemporary Past* (Oxford: Routledge).
—— (2001a), 'Between remembering and forgetting', in V. Buchli and G. Lucas (eds), *Archaeologies of the Contemporary Past* (Oxford: Routledge), 79–83.
Campion Vaughan, E. (1981), *Some Desperate Glory: The Diary of a Young Officer, 1917* (New York (NY): Simon & Schuster).
Cardinal, R. (1994), 'Collecting and Collage-Making: The Case of Kurt Schwitters', in J. Elsner and R. Cardinal (eds), *Cultures of Collecting (Critical Views)* (London: Reaktion Books Ltd), Ch 4.

Castle, I. (1919), *My Husband* (London: John Lane. The Bodley Head).
Chambers, V. (2004), 'A Shell with my Name on it: The Reliance on the Supernatural during the First World War', in D. Evans (ed.), *Journal for the Academic Study of Magic – Issue 2* (Oxford: Mandrake of Oxford), pp. 79–102.
Clark, A. (1999 (1973)), *Aces High. The War in the Air over the Western Front 1914–1918* (London: Cassell & Co.).
Classen, C. (2012), *The Deepest Sense. A Cultural History of Touch* (Urbana (OH), Chicago (IL) and Springfield (IL): University of Illinois Press).
Compston R.J.O. (2009 (1931)), 'The Flight Commander', in E.G. Johnstone (ed.), *Naval Eight. A History of No. 8 Squadron RNAS – afterwards No. 208 Squadron RAF – from formation in 1916 until the Armistice 1918* (Naval & Military Press in association with the Imperial War Museum), 73–103.
Connerton, P. (1989), *How Societies Remember* (Cambridge: Cambridge University Press).
Connor, S. (2010), *The Matter of Air Science and Art of the Ethereal* (London: Reaktion Books).
Cook, T. (2003), 'Dying like so many rats in a trap', *The Army and Doctrine Training Bulletin* 5(4): 47–56.
Copeland Maltby, Paul (1915–16), Personal diary of Captain Paul Copeland Maltby, 15 Squadron RFC, 23 December 1915–24 May 1916. RAF Museum Hendon, AC73/15/2/5.
Cornish, P. and N.J. Saunders (eds) (2014), *Bodies in Conflict. Corporeality, Materiality and Transformation* (London and New York (NY): Routledge).
Crawford, O.G.S. (1921), *Man and His Past* (Oxford: Oxford University Press).
—— (1923), 'Air Survey and Archaeology', *Geographical Journal*, 61(5): 342–60.
—— (1929), *Air Photography for Archaeologists* (London: HMSO).
Crummy, P. (1983), *Colchester Archaeological Report 2; the Roman small finds from excavations in Colchester* (Colchester 1971–9: Colchester Archaeological Trust Ltd).
Csordas, J. (ed.) (1994), *Embodiment and Experience. The Existential Ground of Culture and Self* (Cambridge: Cambridge University Press).
—— (1994a), 'Introduction', in J. Csordas (ed.), *Embodiment and Experience. The Existential Ground of Culture and Self* (Cambridge: Cambridge University Press), 1–24.
D'Alto, N. (2016), 'Inventing the Invisible Airplane. When camouflage was fine art', *Air & Space Magazine* (online), August. Available from: http://airspacemag.com/militaryaviation/art-camouflage-180959768/.
Davies, John William (1987), Interview with John William Davies (recorded and interviewed by Conrad Wood) (IWM Cat. No. 10078), (London: IWM Production Co.) (www.iwm.org.uk/collections/item/object/80009860).
Dendooven, D. (2009), 'The Journey Back. On the nature of donations to the "In Flanders Fields Museum"', in N.J. Saunders and P. Cornish (eds), *Contested Objects. Material Memories of the Great War* (London and New York (NY): Routledge), 60–72.
Douglas, S. (1963), *Years of Combat* (London: Collins).
Downing, H.G. (1916–17), Private documents. IWM Docs 6.
Dunn, M. (1941), 'Some airmen have queer superstitions. Many and quaint are the mascots and talismans adopted, but skill is more important than luck nowadays', *Supplement to*

the Argus (Melbourne), Saturday, 4 October, p. 2 (online). Available from: http://trove.nla.gov.au/ndp/del/article/.

Elsner, J. and R. Cardinal (eds) (1994), *Cultures of Collecting (Critical Views)* (London: Reaktion Books Ltd).

Evans, A.J. (1921), *The Escaping Club* (London: John Lane. The Bodley Head Ltd).

Evans, D. (ed.) (2004), *Journal for the Academic Study of Magic – Issue 2* (Oxford: Mandrake of Oxford).

Farmer, D. (2011), *Oxford Dictionary of Saints* (Oxford: Oxford University Press).

Fawcett, B.C. (2000), 'The Chinese Labour Corps in France 1917–1921', *Journal of the Royal Asiatic Society Hong Kong Branch* (online), 40: 33–111. Available from: www.jstor.org/stable/23895259.

Fitzsimons, P. (2010), *Charles Kingford Smith and Those Magnificent Men* (Australia and New Zealand: Harper Collins).

Formanek-Brunell, M. (ed.) (1997), *The Story of Rose O'Neill: An Autobiography* (Missouri: University of Missouri Press).

Franks, N., H. Giblin and N. McCrery (2007), *Under the Guns of the Red Baron The Complete Record of Von Richtofen's Victories and Victims Fully Illustrated* (London: Grub Street).

Frazer, J.G. (1994 (1911)), *The Golden Bough. A study in magic and religion* (Oxford and New York (NY): Oxford University Press).

Fussell, P. (2000 (1975)), *The Great War and Modern Memory* (Oxford: Oxford University Press).

Gascoyne, J.V. (1972), Interview with James Gascoyne (recorded and interviewed by David G. Lance), 12 January 1972 (IWM Cat. No. 16) (London: IWM Production Co) (www.iwm.org.uk/collections/item/object/80000016).

Geldard, F.A. (1953), *The Human Senses* (New York (NY): John Wiley & Sons Inc.).

Gell, A. (1977), 'Magic, perfume, dream', in I. Lewis (ed.), *Symbols and Sentiments: Cross Cultural Studies in Symbolism* (London and New York (NY): Academic Press), 25–38.

—— (1998), *Art and Agency. An Anthropological Theory* (Oxford and New York (NY): Oxford University Press).

Geurts, K. (2002, Kindle edn), *Culture and the Senses. Bodily Ways of Knowing in an African Community* (Berkeley (CA) and Los Angeles (CA): University of California Press).

Gibson, James J. (1950), *The Perception of the Visual World* (Boston (MA): Houghton Mifflin Company).

—— (1966), *The Senses Considered as a Perceptual System* (Boston (MA): Houghton Mifflin Company).

—— (1986 (1979)), *The Ecological Approach to Visual Perception* (Hillsdale (NJ): Lawrence Erlbaum Associates, Inc.).

Gordon, B. (1986), 'The Souvenir: Messenger of the Extraordinary', *Journal of Popular Culture* (online), 20(3): 135–46. Available from: https://search.proquest.com/docview/1297348759/fulltext/FA8382FC634946B2PQ/1?ac countid=9730.

Gosden, C. (2001), 'Making Sense: Archaeology and Aesthetics', *World Archaeology* (online), 33(2): 163–7. Available from: www.jstor.org/stable/827896.

Gould Lee, A. (1969), *No Parachute. The Exploits of a Fighter Pilot in the First World War* (London: Arrow Books Ltd).
—— (1969a), *Open Cockpit. A Pilot of the Royal Flying Corps* (London: Jarrolds Publishers (London) Ltd).
Granville White, C. (2019), *War Amongst the Clouds. My Flying Experiences in World War I* (London: Grub Street).
Grinnell-Milne, D. (1957 (1933)), *Wind in the Wires* (London: Hamilton & Co. (Stafford) Ltd).
Gwinnell (1919), 'Souvenirs', in Major General H.B. Williams (ed.), *The Golden Horseshoe. Written and Illustrated by Men of the 37th Division B.E.F.* (London, New York, Toronto and Melbourne: Cassell & Company Ltd), 46–7.
Hallam, E. and J. Hockey (2001), *Death, Memory and Material Culture* (Oxford and New York (NY): Berg).
Hammerton, J.A. (ed.) (1914), 'Civilian Curiosity in the Evidences of War 19 December', *The War Illustrated. A Pictorial Record of the Conflict of the Nations, Volume I* (London: The Amalgamated Press Ltd).
Hart, P. (2005), *Bloody April Slaughter in the Skies over Arras, 1917* (London: Cassell).
Helms, M.W. (1988), *Ulysses' Sail: An Ethnographic Odyssey of Power, Knowledge and Geographical Distance* (Princeton (NJ): Princeton University Press).
Hertz, R. (1973 (1909)), 'The pre-eminence of the right hand: a study of religious polarity', in Robert Needham (ed.), *Right and Left: Essays on Dual Symbolic Classification*, tr. R. Needham (Chicago (IL) and London: University of Chicago Press), pp. 3–31.
Hicks, D. and M.C. Beaudry (eds) (2010), *The Oxford Handbook of Material Culture Studies* (Oxford: Oxford University Press).
Hildburgh, W.L. (1951), 'Psychology Underlying the Employment of Amulets in Europe', *Folklore* (online), 62(1): 231–51. Available from: www.jstor.org/stable/1257512.
Hill, J. (2007), 'The Story of the Amulet. Locating the Enchantment of Collections', *Journal of Material Culture* (online), 12(1): 65–87. Available from: http://journals.sagepub.com/doi/abs/10.1177/1359183507074562.
Holt, T. and V. Holt (1996), *Major & Mrs Holt's Battlefield Guide to the Somme* (London: Leo Cooper).
Hopkins, Mayne G. (1972), 'Pusher Pilot with 22. Recollections of 2nd Lt. Geoffrey Mayne Hopkins, 22 Squadron, RFC. With additional narrative and information by Captain H. Rupert Hawkins', *Cross & Cockade Great Britain Journal*, 3(2): 45–57.
Hoskins, J. (1998), *Biographical Objects. How Things Tell the Stories of People's Lives* (London & New York (NY): Routledge).
—— (2006), 'Agency, Biography and Objects', in C. Tilley, W. Keane, S. Küchler, M. Rowlands and P. Spyer (eds), *Handbook of Material Culture* (London: SAGE Publications Ltd), 74–84.
Howes, D. (ed.) (1991), *The Varieties of Sensory Experience* (Toronto: University of Toronto Press).
—— (1991a), 'Introduction. To summon all the senses', in D. Howes (ed.), *The Varieties of Sensory Experience* (Toronto: University of Toronto Press), 3–21.
—— (1991b), 'Sensorial Anthropology', in D. Howes (ed.), *The Varieties of Sensory Experience* (Toronto: University of Toronto Press), 167–91.

Isyanova, G. (2009), *The Consumer Sphinx. From French trench to Parisian market*, in N.J. Saunders and P. Cornish (eds), *Contested Objects. Material Memories of the Great War* (London and New York (NY): Routledge), 130–43.
Johnstone, E.G. (ed.), *Naval Eight. A History of No. 8 Squadron RNAS – afterwards No. 208 Squadron RAF – from formation in 1916 until the Armistice 1918* (Naval & Military Press in association with the Imperial War Museum).
Jones, C.A. (ed.) (2006), *Sensorium. Embodies experience, technology, and contemporary art* (Massachusetts (MA): MIT Press).
Jones, I. (ed.) (1934), *King of Air Fighters. Biography of Major Mick Mannock VC, DSO, MC* (London: Ivor Nicholson & Watson Ltd).
Jünger, E. (2004 (1920)), *Storm of Steel*, tr. M. Hoffmann (London: Penguin Books Ltd).
Kemp, A. (2000), 'Little Red Devil', *Cross & Cockade International Journal*, 31(3): 148–50.
Kimball, J.A. (2004), *Trench Art. An Illustrated History* (California: Silverpenny Press).
Klee, F. (ed.) (1964), *The Diaries of Paul Klee 1898–1918* (Los Angeles (CA) and London: University of California Press).
Kopytoff, I. (1986), 'The cultural biography of things: commoditization as process', in A. Appadurai (ed.), *The social life of things. Commodities in cultural perspective* (Cambridge: Cambridge University Press), 64–91.
Kornerup, A. and J.H. Wanscher (1978), *Methuen Handbook of Colour* (Danish and English edn) (London: Eyre Methuen).
Kwint, M. (1999), 'Introduction', in M. Kwint, C. Breward and J. Aynsley (eds), *Material Memories: Design and Evocation* (Oxford: Berg), 1–16.
Kwint, M., C. Breward and J. Aynsley (eds) (1999), *Material Memories: Design and Evocation* (Oxford: Berg).
Langham, R. (2016, Kindle edn), *Bloody Paralyser. The Giant Handley Page Bombers of the First World War* (UK: Fonthill Media Ltd).
Latour, B. (1993, Kindle edn), *We have Never Been Modern*, tr. C. Porter (Cambridge (MA): Harvard University Press).
—— (2006), 'Air', in C.A. Jones (ed.), *Sensorium. Embodies experience, technology, and contemporary art* (Massachusetts (MA): MIT Press), 105–7.
Lawson, E. and J. Lawson (1996), *Great Air Campaigns. The First Air Campaign August 1914–November 1918* (Cambridge (MA): Da Capo Press).
Leslie, S. (ed.) (1924), *Memoirs of Brigadier-General Gordon Shephard DSO, M.C* (privately printed).
Levine, J. (2008), *On a Wing and a Prayer* (London: Collins).
Lewis, C. (2009 (1936)), *Sagittarius Rising* (Yorkshire: Frontline Books).
—— (1964), *Farewell to Wings* (London: Temple Press Books Ltd).
Lewis, I. (ed.) (1977), *Symbols and Sentiments: Cross Cultural Studies in Symbolism* (London and New York (NY): Academic Press).
Li Ma (ed.) (2012), *Les travailleurs chinois en France dans la Première Guerre mondiale* (Paris: CNRS).
Lidsey, William John (Jack) (1916–17), Private documents. IWM Docs 16504.
Lloyd, D. (1998, Kindle edn), *Battlefield Tourism. Pilgrimage and the Commemoration of the Great War in Britain, Australia and Canada 1919–1939* (London: Bloomsbury).

Lloyd Sproule, Randall Eric (1917–18), Letters to his mother covering the entire period of his service and captivity, from 1 January 1917–4 December 1918. Private documents. RAF Museum Hendon, AC97/69/22.

Lock, G. and B.L. Molyneaux (eds) (2006), *Confronting Scale in Archaeology. Issues of Theory and Practice* (New York (NY): Springer).

Longworth, P. (2010 (1967)), *The Unending Vigil. The History of the Commonwealth War Graves Commission* (Barnsley: Pen & Sword Military).

Loraine, W. (1938), *Robert Loraine. Soldier, Actor, Airman* (London: Collins Publishers).

Lovett, E. (1925), *Magic in Modern London* (Croydon: Advertiser Offices).

—— (1928), *Folklore and Legend of the Surrey Hills and of the Sussex Downs and Forests* (Caterham Valley).

MacCarron, D. (2006), *Letters from an Early Bird – the Life and Letters of Denys Corbett Wilson 1882–1915* (Barnsley: Pen & Sword Aviation).

McCudden VC, James B. (1930 (1918)), *Flying Fury* (London: John Hamilton Ltd).

MacDonagh, M. (1916), 'The Wearing of Religious Emblems at the Front', *Occult Review* (online), XXIV(5): 266–74. Available from: www.iapsop.com/archive/materials/occult_review/occult_review_v24_n5_nov_1 916.pdf.

McHardy, A. (2007 (1918)), *An Airman's Wife: A True Story of Lovers Separated by War* (London: Grub Street).

Maclennan, R.W. (2009), *The Ideals and Training of a Flying Officer* (Manchester: Crécy Publishing Ltd).

Macmillan, N. (2015 (1929), Kindle edn), *Into the Blue* (London: Grub Street).

'McScotch' (1985 (1936)), *Fighter Pilot* (London: Greenhill Books, Lionel Leventhal Ltd).

Malinowski, B. (2015 (1922)), *Argonauts of the Western Pacific. An account of native enterprise and adventure in the Archipelagoes of Melanesian New Guinea* (London and New York (NY): Routledge Classic).

Mauss, M. (1979 (1935)), 'The Notion of Body Techniques', in M. Mauss (ed.), *Sociology and Psychology. Essays*, tr. Ben Brewster (London: Routledge & Kegan Paul), 95–123.

—— (1990 (1954)), *The Gift. The form and reason for exchange in archaic societies*, tr. W.D. Halls (London and New York (NY): Routledge).

—— (ed.) (1979a (1935a)), *Sociology and Psychology. Essays*, tr. Ben Brewster (London: Routledge & Kegan Paul).

Miller, D. (ed.) (1998), *Material cultures: Why some things matter* (London: UCL Press).

—— (1998a), 'Why some things matter', in D. Miller (ed.), *Material cultures: Why some things matter* (London: UCL Press), pp. 3–21.

Molyneaux, B.L. (2006), 'Topographical Scale as Ideological and Practical Affordance: The Case of Devils Tower', in G. Lock and B.L. Molyneaux (eds), *Confronting Scale in Archaeology. Issues of Theory and Practice* (New York (NY): Springer), 67–76.

Montagu, A. (1986 (1971)), *Touching. The Human Significance of the Skin* (New York (NY): Harper).

Morris, D., P. Collett, P. Marsh and M. O'Shaughnessy (1981), *Gestures. Their Origins and Distribution. A New Look at the Human Animal* (London: Triad Granada).

Needham, Robert (ed.) (1973 (1909)), *Right and Left: Essays on Dual Symbolic Classification*, tr. R. Needham (Chicago (IL) and London: University of Chicago Press).

Nettleingham, F.T. (1917), *Tommy's Tunes. Collected and Arranged by 2nd Lt. F.T. Nettleingham, RFC* (London: Erskine Macdonald Ltd).

O'Neill, M. (2016, Kindle edn), *The Chinese Labour Corps: The Forgotten Chinese Labourers of the First World War* (London: Penguin).

Orpen, W. (1921), *An Onlooker in France 1917–1919* (London: Williams & Norgate).

Ortweiler, Frederick J. (1917), Diary written during service as wireless operator with Royal Flying Corps on Western Front. April–May 1917. Private documents. RAF Museum Hendon, AC88/73.

Paine, S. (2004), *Amulets. World of Secret Powers, Charms and Magic* (London: Thames & Hudson).

Paterson, M. (2007, Kindle edn), *The Senses of Touch. Haptics, Affects and Technologies* (Oxford and New York (NY): Berg).

Pels, P. (2010), 'Magical things: on fetishes, commodities, and computers', in D. Hicks and M. Beaudry (eds), *The Oxford Handbook of Material Culture Studies* (Oxford: Oxford University Press), 613–33.

Pink, S. (2009), *Doing Sensory Ethnography* (London: Sage Publications).

Poulbot, F. (1917), *Encores des Gosses et des Bonhommes: cent dessins et l'Histoire de Nénette et Rintintin* (Paris: A. Ternois).

Pulteney, Sir William and B. Brice (1925), *The Immortal Salient. An Historical Record and Complete Guide for Pilgrims to Ypres* (London: John Murray for the Ypres League).

Raleigh, Sir Walter (1922), *The War in the Air. Being the Story of the Part played in the Great War by the Royal Air Force. Vol. I* (Oxford: Clarendon Press).

Ralph, W. (1999), *Barker VC. The Classic Story of a Legendary First World War Hero* (London: Grub Street).

Rewald, S. (1988), *Paul Klee* (New York (NY): Metropolitan Museum of Art).

Rivlin, R. and K. Gravelle (1984), *Deciphering the Senses. The Expanding World of Human Perception* (New York (NY): Simon & Schuster).

Roberts, D. (2003), Letter: 'Barker's fin', *Windsock International*, 19(1): 2.

Rodaway, P. (1994), *Sensuous Geographies. Body, Sense and Place* (London and New York (NY): Routledge).

Roud, S. (2006), *The Penguin Guide to the Superstitions of Britain and Ireland* (London: Penguin Books).

Roure, L. (1917), 'Superstitions du front de guerre', *Edtudes*, 153: 710–11.

Routh, Wing Commander, E.J.D. (n.d.), Private documents. IWM Docs 20671.

Ruan, X. (1996), 'Empowerment in the Practice of Making and Inhabiting. Dong Architecture in Cultural Reconstruction', *Journal of Material Culture* (online), 1(2): 211–37, p. 217. Available from: http://journals.sagepub.com.bris.idm.oclc.org/doi/pdf/10.1177/135918359600100204.

Saunders, N.J. (1999), 'Biographies of Brilliance: Pearls, Transformations of Matter and being c. AD 1492', *World Archaeology* (online), 31(2): 243–57. Available from: www.jstor.org/stable/125060.

—— (2001). 'Apprehending memory: material culture and war 1919–1939', in J. Bourne, P. Liddle and I. Whitehead (eds), *The Great World War 1914–45, Volume 2, The peoples' experience* (London: HarperCollins Publishers), 476–88.

—— (2002), 'Bodies of Metal, Shells of Memory: "Trench Art" and the Great War Recycled', in V. Buchli (ed.), *The material culture reader* (Oxford and New York (NY): Berg), 181–206.

—— (2002a), 'Memory and Conflict', in V. Buchli (ed.), *The material culture reader* (Oxford and New York: Berg), 175–80.

—— (2003), *Trench Art. Materialities and Memories of War* (Oxford and New York (NY): Berg).

—— (ed.) (2004), *Matters of Conflict. Material Culture, Memory and the First World War* (London and New York (NY): Routledge).

—— (2004a), 'Material Culture and Conflict. The Great War, 1914–2003', in N.J. Saunders (ed.), *Matters of Conflict. Material Culture, Memory and the First World War* (London and New York (NY): Routledge), 5–25.

—— (2007), *Killing Time. Archaeology and the First World War* (Stroud: Sutton Publishing Ltd).

—— (2009), 'People in Objects: Individuality and the Quotidian in the Material Culture War', in C.L. White (ed.), *The Materiality of Individuality. Archaeological Studies of Individual Lives* (London and New York (NY): Springer Dordrecht Heidelberg), 37–55.

—— (ed.) (2012), *Beyond the Dead Horizon. Studies in Modern Conflict Archaeology* (Oxford: Oxbow Books).

—— (2012a), 'Travail et nostalgie sur le front de l'Ouest: l'Art des tranchées chinois et la Première guerre mondiale', in Li Ma (ed.), *Les travailleurs chinois en France dans la Première Guerre mondiale* (Paris: CNRS), 435–51.

—— (2014), 'Bodies in Trees. A matter of being in Great War landscapes', in P. Cornish and N.J. Saunders (eds), *Bodies in Conflict. Corporeality, Materiality and Transformation* (London and New York (NY): Routledge), 22–38.

—— (2016), '"Pearl's Treasure": The Trench Art Collection of an Australian Sapper', in L. Slade (ed.), *Sappers and Shrapnel: Contemporary Art and the Art of the Trenches* (Adelaide: Art Gallery of South Australia), 13–27.

Saunders, N.J. and P. Cornish (eds) (2009), *Contested Objects. Material Memories of the Great War* (London and New York (NY): Routledge).

Saunders, N.J. and P. Cornish (2009a), 'Introduction', in N.J. Saunders and P. Cornish (eds), *Contested Objects. Material Memories of the Great War* (London and New York (NY): Routledge), 1–10.

Scarry, E. (1985), *The Body in Pain. The Making and Unmaking of the World* (Oxford: Oxford University Press).

Seremetakis, C.N. (ed.) (1994), *The Senses Still: Perception and Memory as Material Culture in Modernity* (Chicago (IL) and London: University of Chicago Press).

—— (1994a), 'The Memory of the Senses, Part I: Marks of the Transitory', in C.N. Seremetakis (ed.), *The Senses Still: Perception and Memory as Material Culture in Modernity* (Chicago (IL) and London: University of Chicago Press), 1–18.
Seton Hutchison, G. (1936), *Pilgrimage* (London: Rich & Cowan Ltd).
Sharper Knowlson, T. (1934 (1910)), *The Origins of Popular Superstitions and Customs* (London: T. Werner Laurie Ltd).
Shores, C., N. Franks and R. Guest (1990), *Above the Trenches. A Complete Record of the Fighter Aces and Units of the British Empire and Air Forces 1915–1920* (London: Grub Street).
Skelton, M.L. (1977), 'Captain Vernon Castle Royal Flying Corps', *Cross & Cockade Great Britain Journal*, 8(2): 62–73.
—— (1979), 'Lt. Roy Shillinglaw recalls 100 Squadron', *Cross & Cockade Great Britain Journal*, 10(3): 114–20.
Slade, L. (ed.) (2016), *Sappers and Shrapnel: Contemporary Art and the Art of the Trenches* (Adelaide: Art Gallery of South Australia).
Sloterdijk, P. (2009 (2002)), *Terror from the Air* (Los Angeles (LA): Semiotext(e)).
Smart, C. (1916–17), Diary. Private documents. RAF Museum London, AC98/31/69.
Snape, M.F. and S.G. Parker (2001), 'Keeping faith and coping: belief, popular religiosity and the British people', in J. Bourne, P. Liddle and I. Whitehead (eds), *The Great World War 1914–45, Volume 2 The peoples' experience* (London: HarperCollins Publishers), 397–420.
Stewart, S. (1993), *On Longing. Narratives of the Miniature, the Gigantic, the Souvenir, the Collection* (Durham (NC) and London: Duke University Press).
Strange, L.A. (1935), *Recollections of an Airman* (London: John Hamilton Ltd).
Strenski, I. (1992 (1922)), *Malinowski and the Work of Myth* (Princeton (NJ): Princeton University Press).
Tarlow, S. (1999), *Bereavement and Commemoration. An Archaeology of Mortality* (Oxford: Blackwell Publishers).
—— (2000), 'Emotion in Archaeology', *Current Anthropology* (online), 41(5): 713–46. Available from: www.jstor.org/stable/10.1086/317404.
Taylor, G. (1968), *Sopwith Scout 7309* (London: Cassell & Co. Ltd).
Thom, T. (1987), *The Air Pilot's Manual. Volume 1: Flying Training* (Shrewsbury: Airlife Publishing Ltd).
Thomas, W. and K. Pavitt (1914), *The Book of Talismans, Amulets and Zodiacal Gems* (London: William Rider & Son Ltd).
Thrift, N. (2010), 'Afterword: Fings ain't wot they used t'be: thinking through material thinking as placing and arrangement', in D. Hicks and M.C. Beaudry (eds), *The Oxford Handbook of Material Culture Studies* (Oxford: Oxford University Press).
Tilley, C., W. Keane, S. Küchler, M. Rowlands and P. Spyer (eds) (2006), *Handbook of Material Culture* (London: SAGE Publications Ltd).
Turner, E.S. (1980), *Dear Old Blighty* (London: Michael Joseph Ltd).
Vann, R. (1978), 'Nine months with 5 Squadron RFC. The recollections of Captain Herman Lloyd Tracy as told to Raymond Vann', *Cross & Cockade Great Britain Journal*, 9(1): 23–4.

Velasco, G. (2010), *Fighting Colours: The Creation of Military Aircraft Nose Art* (Tennessee: Turner Publishing Company).

Villiers, E. (1929), *The Mascot Book* (London: T. Werner Laurie Ltd).

Vinge, L. (1975), *The Five Senses: Studies in a Literary Tradition* (Lund: The Royal Society of Letters).

Waite, M. (ed.) (2012 (1979)), *Oxford English Dictionary* (paperback) (Oxford: Oxford University Press).

Wall, G. (1919), *Letters of an Airman* (Melbourne: The Speciality Press Pty, Ltd).

Wallis Budge, Sir E.A. (1968), *Amulets and Talismans* (New York (NY): University Books).

Walton, L. (2010), 'Snapshots from France, 1917–1923', *Channel Islands Great War Study Group Journal* (online), 30 February. Available from: www.greatwarci.net/journals/30.pdf.

Ward-Jackson, C.H. (ed.) (1945), *Airman's Song Book* (London: Sylvan Press).

Watson, A. (2006), 'Self-deception and survival: Mental Coping Strategies on the Western Front, 1914–18', *Journal of Contemporary History* (online), 41(2): 247–68. Available from: www.jstor.org/stable/30036385.

Wenzel, M. and J. Cornish (1980), *Auntie Mabel's War. An account of her part in the hostilities of 1914–1918* (London: Allen Lane).

White, C.L. (ed.) (2009), *The Materiality of Individuality. Archaeological Studies of Individual Lives* (London and New York (NY): Springer Dordrecht Heidelberg).

Williams, MC DFC, Captain F. (2019), *Don't let them Bag the Nines. The First World War Memoir of a de Havilland Pilot* (Cheltenham: The History Press).

Williams, Major General H.B. (ed.) (1919), *The Golden Horseshoe. Written and Illustrated by Men of the 37th Division B.E.F.* (London, New York (NY), Toronto and Melbourne: Cassell & Company Ltd).

Williamson, H. (2009 (1929), Kindle edn), *The Wet Flanders Plain* (London: Faber & Faber).

Winter, J. (2006), *Remembering War. The Great War between Memory and History in the Twentieth Century* (New Haven (CT) and London: Yale University Press).

Winterton, M. (2012), 'Signs, Signals and Senses: the soldier body in the trenches', in N.J. Saunders (ed.), *Beyond the Dead Horizon. Studies in Modern Conflict Archaeology* (Oxford: Oxbow Books), 229–41.

Woodcock, T. and J.M. Robinson (2001 (1988)), *The Oxford Guide to Heraldry* (New York (NY): Oxford University Press).

Wordsworth, W. (1984 (1807)), *Wordsworth's Poems in Two Volumes (1807): A Facsimile* (London: British Library).

Wortley, Rothesay S. (1982 (1928)), *Letters from a Flying Officer* (Gloucester: Alan Sutton Publishing Ltd).

Wright, A.R. and E. Lovett (1908), 'Specimens of Modern Mascots and Ancient Amulets of the British Isles', *Folklore* (online), 19(3): 288–303. Available from: www.jstor.org/stable/1254514.

Wyschogrod (1981), 'Empathy and Sympathy as Tactile Encounter', *Journal of Medicine and Philosophy*, 6(1): 25–43.

Yuille, Archibald B. (1973), Experiences of a Royal Flying Corps pilot 1917–1918. Interview with A. Yuille (recorded and interviews by D. Lance), 4 June 1973 (IWM Cat. No. 4267) (London: IWM Production Co.) (www.iwm.org.uk/collections/item/object/80000319).

Websites

'A Church near you' – www.achurchnearyou.com/twineham-st-peter/.
Australian War Memorial Museum: Hay – www.awm.gov.au/collection/C289714.
Australian War Memorial Museum: Marston – www.awm.gov.au/collection/REL33984/.
Aviation archive (u.d.) 'Women Doping Wings' – www.aviationarchive.org.uk/Gpages/html/G2083.html.
Bible Gateway Psalm 91 – www.biblegateway.com/passage/?search=Psalm+91&version=KJV.
Commonwealth War Graves Commission 'About Us' – www.cwgc.org/about-us.
Commonwealth War Graves Commission: Corbett Wilson and Woodiwiss – www.cwgc.org/find-war-dead/casualty/585327/corbett-wilson,- denys/#&gid=null&pid=1.
Commonwealth War Graves Commission: Menin Gate – www.cwgc.org/find/find-cemeteries-and-memorials/91800/ypres-memorial).
Crutchley, G. (u.d.), 'My grandfather' – www.flyingclothing.co.uk/pg005.html.
Irish Linen Centre & Lisburn Museum: 'Aerolinen – The War was Won on Ulster Wings' – www.lisburnmuseum.com/2014/08/the-war-was-won-on-ulster-linen-wings-howaerolinen-and-andrews-mill-in-comber-aided-the-war-effort/.
National Museum of Wales – https://museum.wales/collections/online/?field0=string&value0=edward lovett collection mascots&field1=with_images&value1=on&page=1.
Oxford Dictionary of National Biography – www.oxforddnb.com/view/article/68195?docPos=3).
'The Returned from the Front' – http://thereturned.co.uk/the-grave-markers/.
Tuck DB Postcards, History of R. Tuck and Sons Ltd – http://tuckdb.org/history.
University of Sydney, Roll of Service, p. 215 – http://beyond1914.sydney.edu.au/profile/3126/john-hay.
War History Online War History Online – www.warhistoryonline.com/war-articles/relatives-red-baron-albert-ball-meetroyal-air-force-museum.html.

Index

aerial photography xi, 6, 19, 25, 27, 31, 33, 44, 70
    oblique photograph 6, 25
    vertical photograph 31
Allingham, Henry 69
Archie 27, 40, 68, 105
    as lucky pocket piece 60
Arkell, Lieutenant Anthony 83, 102, 103
Arras 28, 89, 91, 92
    Cathedral 118
    Flying Services Memorial 105, 118
Ashwin, Lieutenant Guy 89

Balfour, Harold 4, 14
Ball VC, DSO, MC, Flight Commander Captain Albert 68
Baring, Maurice 4, 62, 93, 101
Barker, Major William 114–16
Bond, Captain William 8, 104–6
Bott, Alan 8, 9, 17, 27, 37
Brancker, Major General W.S. 9

Castle, Captain Vernon 19, 20, 25, 27, 54, 69–71, 110, 122
Chinese Labour Corps 119
Comber-Taylor, Captain Eric Horace 95
Copeland Maltby, Captain Paul 19
Corbett Wilson, Lieutenant Denys 17, 22, 44, 88
Crawford, O.G.S. 6
Crutchley, Gerard Gwyn 59
Cutler, Lieutenant H.C. 96–7

Davies, John William 23, 38–9
Douglas, Sholto 4, 32, 80, 81
Downing, 2nd Lieutenant H.G. 22, 25

Ely, 2nd Lieutenant Frank Wayman 117–18
Evans, Lieutenant A.J. 31

flying ace 7, 8, 41, 91–2

Gascoyne, James V. 23
Gould Lee, Arthur 5, 20–1, 24, 29, 32, 35–6, 45, 48–9, 65, 102, 116
Granville White, Hugh 4, 21–2
Grinnell-Milne, Duncan 8, 65, 76, 81, 104, 108, 113

Handley Page 52, 62–3, 83, 113, *see also* night flying
    Black Cat Squadron 63
    nose art 114
haptic 11, 13, 45
    activities 17, 25, 27
    emotions 45
    experience 10–11, 13, 19, 27
    kinaesthesia 24
    senses 13, 27, 34, 36
    space 19
    tactics 24, 30
    thresholds 35
    verification 27
    vestibular sense 19, 25

vibration 27–8, 34
visual kinesthesis 31

Hay, John 78–80
Hendon Aerodrome 23
Hopkins, 2nd Lieutenant Mayne G. 40
Hucks Small, Lieutenant B.C. 60–1

Klee, P. 116, 117

Lewis, C. 23, 30, 34, 40, 42, 84
Lidsey, Lieutenant William John (Jack) 9
Lloyd Sproule, Randall Eric 58
Lloyd Tracy, Captain Herman 27
Loraine, Lieutenant Robert 61, 71

McCudden VC, Major James B. 7, 9, 21, 28, 61, 91, 101, 103–4
McGavock Grider, John 8, 14, 45, 48, 58, 60, 64, 107
MacLanachan, William 64, 105
Maclennan, Roderick Ward 17, 24
Macmillan, Norman 65–7, 106–7
'McScotch', No. 43 Squadron 64, 105, see also MacLanachan, William 64, 105
Mannock VC, DSO, MC, Major Mick 81
Marston, Henry James 55
mascot, definition 47–8
Menin Gate Memorial to the Missing 93
Messines Ridge, Battle of 104
Mitchel-Clarke, Major Alfred John 68

night flying 32, 34, 52, 62–3, 83, 103, 113, see also Handley Page

Orpen, Major Sir William 82
Ortweiler, Frederick J. 23, 37, 48

Rickenbacker, Captain Eddie 69
Richthofen, Manfred von 41, 59–60, 79–80, 101
Routh, Wing Commander Eric 21

Saint-Omer 5, 6, 19, 90–1, 92
Schwitters, Kurt 117
Shephard, Brigadier General Gordon 85–7
Shillinglaw, 2nd Lieutenant Roy 62–3
Smart, Lieutenant Charles 28
Somme 1916, Battle of the 13, 27, 31, 70
Stagg, Private A.T.C. 83, 103
Stockton Smith, Lieutenant Leonard 104
Strange, Lieutenant Colonel L.A. 42–3, 80
superstition, definition 45–6

Taylor, Gordon 4, 18, 20–1, 24, 35, 60, 65–7, 68, 101
Trenchard, Air Marshal Sir Hugh 62, 87
trench art
    authenticity 122
    definition 15

Wall, Geoffrey, pilot RFC 8, 18, 22, 35, 48, 53, 71
White Springs, Elliot 8
Willey, Corporal J. 106–7
Williams MC DFC, Captain F. 45, 88
Worcestershire Yeomanry, Museum of 96
Wortley, Rothesay S. 30
Wright, Orville and Wilbur 4

Ypres 93–4, 101, 106–7, 121
    Third Battle of 107
Yuille, Archibald B. 34